How to Pass

EDITION

HIGHER

Computing Science

Greg Reid

HODDER
GIBSON
AN HACHETTE UK COMPANY

The Publishers would like to thank the following for permission to reproduce copyright material.

Photo credits
p.5 composite created with images by © vladstar/stock.adobe.com and © PiyawatNandeenoparit/stock.adobe.com; **p.9** © rukawajung/stock.adobe.com; **p.38** © ifeelstock/Alamy Stock Photo; **p.48** © Getty Images/Thinkstock/iStockphoto/fuchs-photography; **p.50** © Getty Images/Thinkstock/iStockphoto/fuchs-photography; **p.52** © Greg Reid **p.55** top © Jesper Jørgen Fotografi ApS © All rights reserved for VELUX; bottom © Hive Energy.

Acknowledgements

Every effort has been made to trace all copyright holders, but if any have been inadvertently overlooked, the Publishers will be pleased to make the necessary arrangements at the first opportunity.

Orders: please contact Bookpoint Ltd, 130 Park Drive, Milton Park, Abingdon, Oxon OX14 4SE. Telephone: (44) 01235 827827.
Fax: (44) 01235 400454. Email: education@bookpoint.co.uk. Lines are open from 9 a.m. to 5 p.m., Monday to Friday, with a 24-hour message answering service. Visit our website at www.hoddereducation.co.uk. If you have queries or questions that aren't about an order you can contact us at hoddergibson@hodder.co.uk.

© Greg Reid 2019

First published in 2015 © Greg Reid
This second edition published in 2019 by
Hodder Gibson, an imprint of Hodder Education
An Hachette UK Company
211 St Vincent Street
Glasgow, G2 5QY

Impression number   5   4   3   2
Year   2023 2022 2021 2020

Cover photo © Aliaksandra - stock.adobe.com
Illustrations by Aptara, Inc.
Typeset in CronosPro-Lt 13/15 pts by Aptara, Inc.
Printed in India
A catalogue record for this title is available from the British Library.

ISBN: 978 1 5104 5243 5

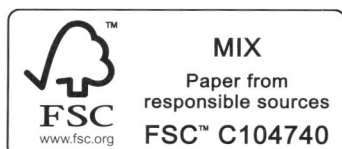

MIX
Paper from responsible sources
FSC™ C104740
FSC
www.fsc.org

SCOTLAND EXCEL
We are an approved supplier on the Scotland Excel framework.

Schools can find us on their procurement system as:
Hodder & Stoughton Limited t/a Hodder Gibson.

Contents

Introduction

Exam preparation

By the time they sit a Higher, many students already know what study methods work for them and what it takes to be successful. You may have passed National 5 Computing Science, but it is important to understand that the step up to Higher is demanding and that you may require a different approach (or approaches) to ensure your success. Read on carefully: you might just find the perfect study tip that makes the difference between one grade and the next.

Course outline

The Higher Computing Science course is split into four 'areas' of study, each of which makes up the following percentage of the course:

- Software Design and Development (SDD) – 40%
- Computer Systems (CS) – 10%
- Database Design and Development (DDD) – 25%
- Web Design and Development (WDD) – 25%.

While all four areas include theory knowledge, only SDD, DDD and WDD also contain practical work.

The three practical areas are further organised into the same development order:

- analysis
- design
- implementation
- testing
- evaluation.

Course assessment

Your final grade is calculated from your success in two components which together total 160 marks. These two components are the exam paper and the assignment.

The exam paper

Length: 2 hours 30 minutes

Marks: 110

- Section 1: short stand-alone questions (25 marks). The majority of questions will range between 1 and 3 marks.
- Section 2: longer questions based around a scenario (85 marks). Each question will have multiple parts (a, bi, bii, c, etc.).

Note that Computer Systems will be assessed entirely by the exam paper as there is no practical element that could be assessed. This means that approximately 16 marks (10% of the total 160 marks) of the exam paper will be questions on Computer Systems.

The assignment

Length: 8 hours

Marks: 50

The assignment is split into three tasks: one task each for the three practical areas of SDD, DDD and WDD.

While each task can potentially cover any part of the development process from analysis to design, in reality the marks will be spread across the three tasks. The specimen task published by SQA has the following breakdown of marks.

	Task 1: DDD	Task 2: SDD	Task 3: WDD	Totals
Analysis		2	3	**5**
Design	3		2	**5**
Implementation	7	15	8	**30**
Testing	2	3		**5**
Evaluation		5		**5**
				(50)

Each year the marks will be split differently across the tasks but the totals shown for each step of the development process will always remain the same (5, 5, 30, 5 and 5).

Note that most of the marks in the assignment are allocated to Implementation. This means that writing code will be mainly assessed in the assignment rather than in the exam paper.

The basics of revising

How many of the ideas below have you incorporated in your studying?
- Consider the grade you want to achieve. It's important to have a target.
- Devise a study plan and stick to it. Don't let yourself get distracted. Half an hour of focused, uninterrupted work is much more effective than two hours spent revising while texting and checking social media.
- Consider what you can do without. Effective study is time consuming. Is finding out who has died in your favourite soap as important as getting the grades for the college or university place you want?
- Look after yourself. Sleep well, eat well and avoid other stressful situations. Studying and exams can be stressful enough.
- Find out as much as you can about the exam and practise for it. This book will help you with this.
- Know your course. The SQA publishes course outlines for teachers; these can be accessed by anyone. You can use the outline as a checklist of what you have to learn. The list can be found on pages 4–12 of the Course Specification document at www.sqa.org.uk.

Why use practice exam questions?

The famous Chinese philosopher Confucius said, 'The essence of knowledge is, having it, to apply it; not having it, to confess your ignorance.'

Too many students spend an inordinate amount of time while preparing for an exam applying the knowledge they already have. They sit and read notes they understand, answer questions that they already know the answers to and fail to acknowledge their ignorance of large parts of their course. Take this approach and you will do very well in a small part of your exam only.

The focus of any revision should be to discover what you don't know and to use that as your starting point. Take note of the practice exam and past paper questions that you can't answer quickly; these will show you what you don't know and therefore what you should research as part of your study.

Understanding the course

Don't leave it too late! To understand a course at Higher level often requires you to understand one fact fully before you move on to the next. If you leave a lesson confused, do something about it. Read over your notes again in the evening, ask your teacher for further explanation, attend study groups, use the internet for research or even ask your friends for help. Whichever route you take, make sure that you get into this habit early on in the year.

Memorise, memorise, memorise!

Exams require that you retain knowledge throughout the year, meaning that an ability to memorise facts is vital. Don't simply read your notes when you study. Research has shown that very few people can read text and remember all of it.

It is difficult to advise students on memory techniques. Everyone has different ways of remembering facts so you'll have to find something that works for you. Different memory techniques work for different types of learners.

- Reading/writing preference learners: Take your own notes, summarising the work you have learned in class. Personalising the work often makes it easier to remember.
- Visual learners: Draw diagrams or create concept maps to link facts together in your head.
- Auditory learners: Dictate notes into a recording device and listen to the recordings regularly. Many smartphones have apps to record voice notes.
- Kinaesthetic learners: Practise practical work. For example, writing programs rather than reading code may greatly improve your ability to understand a coding question in an exam.

There are many websites with hundreds of techniques to try. You'll know you've found techniques that work for you when the standard of your work improves.

Focus on problem solving

A Computing Science exam comprises two question types:

1 Knowledge and Understanding (KU) – These are questions that ask you simply to write down or explain a fact or skill you have learned. The current course has only a few of these types of questions in the exam paper.

2 Problem Solving (PS) – These are questions where you are required to apply your knowledge to an unfamiliar scenario. The current course places a great deal of emphasis on you being able to interpret and solve problems in both the assignment and exam paper.

KU questions can be prepared for easily by simply memorising lots of facts.

PS questions require practice. Work through as many unseen exam questions as you can. Design and implement programs, databases and websites as this is a problem-solving exercise in itself.

Questions

Note that the questions in this book have been written in a style that may not always resemble those in the Higher exam. The questions have been created to encourage good study, develop problem solving and practise researching. It is recommended that students apply their revision to past paper or sample paper questions as part of their overall revision plan.

And finally …

Commit!

The most pleasing results for teachers are not necessarily the students who get the A-grade passes. It's often the students who simply achieve their potential through hard work, even if that is just scraping a pass. Every year teachers see a few students who 'could have done better'. Don't let that be you!

Good luck!

Area 1 Software Design and Development

Chapter 1
Development methodologies

A **methodology** refers to a specific technique adopted by developers to design and develop new programs. In the National 5 course you learned about the traditional 'iterative software development cycle' also known as the **waterfall method**. In this methodology the developer works through the following development phases from start to finish:

- analysis
- design
- implementation
- testing
- evaluation.

At times during the software development cycle, it may be necessary to return to a previous step in the cycle. For example, when testing finds an error, part of a program may have to be redesigned and then implemented again. This is known as an **iteration**. The waterfall method is now rarely used in industry. A methodology that takes an entire project, as a whole, from start to finish simply lacks flexibility.

Waterfall has been replaced by a variety of methodologies known collectively as '**agile**'. Agile development aims to follow the same phases as before but breaks a project down into smaller sub-projects. Each sub-project will be independently designed, implemented and tested over a much shorter time-scale. These sub-projects are worked on by small teams, often simultaneously.

Comparing agile and the iterative software development cycle (waterfall)

Agile may be compared to the waterfall method using the criteria given in Table 1.1.

Table 1.1 Comparing agile and waterfall

	Waterfall	**Agile**
Interaction between the client and the developer	During the analysis stage of the waterfall method, the client has a lot of contact with the developer. The developer will gather extensive information from the client through interviews and documentation with the purpose of agreeing an accurate project specification. After their initial contact, there is little client involvement until the finished software is evaluated by both client and developer to agree that the project specification has been met.	During agile development the client may be involved constantly in the development cycle. Each sub-project will create prototypes of the software which the client will be invited to give feedback on. Any required changes are quickly built into the sub-project goals. By involving the client throughout the process, it is far more likely that the client will be happy with the finished software.
Teamwork of different project personnel	As the iterative software development cycle progresses, the project is passed from group to group: systems analysts to programmers then to testers. Each group will work in isolation, only communicating when the project progresses or iteration is required.	Each agile sub-project team will include a range of personnel with expertise in different areas. Constant communication is required if a sub-project team is to meet its short development deadlines and adapt its task according to client feedback. To aid communication, agile teams often work in very close proximity.
Documentation produced	The waterfall method seeks to reduce the need for iteration through increased paperwork and planning. The more detailed the project specification, program design and test plans, the less likely that these phases will need to be revisited. As a consequence, a great deal of documentation is generated. Advocates of this methodology will argue that increased planning will save time later.	Agile views documentation very differently. Many of the documents that the waterfall method focuses on are never subsequently used or updated once the project is finished. Agile reduces the emphasis on documentation. Initial planning is reduced as well as planning and design during the short cycles of sub-projects. Agile regards constant adaptation and change as part of the development process and not something to be feared or reduced through over planning. To create a detailed design that must then be stringently adhered to goes against the very ethos of agile. The documentation produced in agile focuses purely on what is required to keep the project moving towards completion.

Table 1.1 (*continued*)

Measuring the progress of a project	As part of the initial project specification documentation, the waterfall method will include a detailed timeline for each phase of the project. The development team will be measured against their ability to meet these deadline dates.	Agile development works to deadlines for each sub-project during which teams of multi-skilled personnel will complete: ● analysis ● design ● implementation ● unit testing ● acceptance testing. Progress is measured against an overarching deadline for the whole project and whether or not the prototypes developed by the sub-project teams are completed on time. Agile aims to produce sub-projects and the complete program as quickly as possible.
Adaptive or predictive?	A predictive methodology like the waterfall method focuses on spending more time and effort on the initial phases of the project. The thinking behind this is that problems can be predicted and therefore avoided if due diligence is given to detailed analysis and design. A predictive methodology finds it difficult to react to change when it is required. In some cases a 'change control board', made up of staff involved with the project, will meet to make decisions on whether a change is necessary. This ensures that only essential changes to the original plan are ever implemented. A predictive methodology will have clear deadlines mapped out for each phase of development from the beginning of a project.	An adaptive methodology, like agile, can respond to change quickly because the sub-teams contain all the required skills to carry out any new design and implementation. Agile teams are used to working to short time-scales and have no fear of change as it is regarded as an expected part of development. Communication within a sub-team, who are often in the same room, is faster than having to communicate with other staff. Decisions are therefore made quickly, further enhancing the ability of the team to adapt to change. With adaptive methodologies, staff have a good idea of what they are working on tomorrow. The further away a date is, however, the more unlikely it is that sub-team members will be able to supply any detail regarding their tasks for that day. Managers will maintain an overview of sub-projects and ensure deadlines for the project as a whole are met.
Project testing phase	In the waterfall method, carefully planned testing takes place after the program has been implemented. A fault discovered during testing will result in an iteration back to the design or implementation phases.	There is no recognised testing phase in agile development as this is carried out throughout program development while each individual prototype is developed and as prototypes come together to make the finished product. In agile development, constant small iterations take place as program components are built, tested and adapted following feedback from the client.

What you should know 👍

In your revision of this chapter, ensure that you are able to:

★ describe and compare the waterfall method of software development with agile development
★ explain the general principles of agile software development
★ describe the advantages of agile software development over the traditional waterfall method of developing software
★ explain the different relationships between the developer and the client in both types of methodology.

Questions ❓

1 Describe one advantage for the client if a software company uses agile methodologies to develop their product. (1)
2 In any development it is important to plan ahead. Describe the differences in forward planning between the waterfall method and agile methodologies. (2)
3 Explain why only the waterfall development method has a distinct testing phase. (1)
4 Explain why agile methodologies create substantially less documentation when developing software. (1)
5 During software development, changes are sometimes made to designs. State who decides which changes should be implemented for both waterfall and agile development. (2)

Chapter 2
Software analysis

The first phase of any software development project involves clearly defining the software that will be produced.

Software is either produced by a developer for a client (for example, a factory requiring software to control a new device they have manufactured) or produced by a developer for their own financial gain (such as a new leisure game for a phone). Either way, analysis will include outlining the following:

- **Purpose** – This describes the reason for creating new software and may include an identified need of a client and their users. If the developer is creating the software for their own use, or to sell, the needs of the end-user or target audience will become the purpose of creating the software. Understanding and clearly describing what any new software will do is important as it helps inform further analysis and design.
- **Scope** – The scope of the project will include a list of what will be delivered to the client or end-user at the conclusion of the project. This includes the time-scale in which the project will be carried out. In addition to the software itself, a client may expect to receive a report on the test plan, the results of the testing and an evaluation report.

Figure 2.1 Clients can expect to receive reports about their project

- **Boundaries** – This provides a list of what will and won't be included in the project. Without boundaries, the developer and client may disagree about the extent of the project during development. If the client asks for additional functionality during the project, the developer will be able to state that this was not part of the initial contract and may request additional payment to implement the new software features.

- **Functional requirements** – This outlines the project in terms of inputs, processes and outputs. The processes may be listed as the different functions performed by the software.

Worked example

The Music Venue app

A music venue would like to develop a phone application. The app will be used to provide audience members with a set list (including song times) for concerts taking place at the venue. The app will also display when the concert will start and finish.

Figure 2.2

Table 2.1 Worked example of a project specification

Analysis	
Purpose	The purpose of the program (mobile phone application) is to provide audience members at concerts with an easy way to access a list of all the songs being played at a selected concert. The program will also use the information entered for each song to calculate an estimated time for when the concert will finish.
	A title, song information and start time for each concert may be entered by either the organisers of the concert or the band that is performing. To enter this information, a password will be required.
	Any user of the program will be able to search for a concert title and view the information for that concert.
Scope	At the end of this project the client will be supplied with:
	• a program design showing the program's structure
	• a comprehensive test plan for the program
	• a report detailing the results of testing
	• the completed mobile app
	• an evaluation report showing that the agreed project specification has been met.
	The program will be written and tested using modular code and will be designed, written and tested within 20 hours.

⇨

Table 2.1 *(continued)*

Boundaries	The program will store the information for each concert within a .csv file.
	The information for each concert will be:
	• a title for the concert (e.g. 'The Novemberists')
	• the number of songs on the set list (e.g. 14)
	• each song name and a length of time in minutes and seconds (e.g. '"Going Up", 03:57')
	• a starting time for the concert (e.g. '21:10:00').
	A concert will have no more than 25 songs.
	It will be assumed that no two concerts will have the same title.
	The concert information may not be changed once it has been entered.
	The concert information will never be deleted once entered.
	The password required to enter the details for a new concert will be 'GR6168'.
	When the user searches for a concert, the information displayed will be limited to the names of each song, the start time of the concert and the estimated finishing time for the concert.
	The program will run once, first asking if a new concert is to be stored and then asking the user for the name of a concert to display.
Functional requirements	Information for previous concerts will be input from a .csv file.
	Information for a new concert will be entered using the touchscreen keyboard.
	A selected concert will be displayed on the touchscreen.
	The program will run automatically when started.
	Each process identified will be written as a procedure or function.
	Inputs:
	• concert title
	• number of songs in the concert
	• name and duration of each song
	• start time.
	Processes:
	• write new concert's data to the end of a .csv file
	• read previous concert data from the .csv file
	• find a user-selected concert in the file data
	• calculate the finishing time for the selected concert
	• display the information for the selected concert.
	Outputs:
	• concert title, song names, song times and start time for new concert written to file
	• song names, start time and finish time displayed on screen.

The purpose, scope, boundaries and functional requirements together make up the project specification. Where the software is being developed for a client, this will form the basis of a contract between developer and client. The developer has outlined what they will create and the client understands what they can expect to receive when the project is complete.

What you should know 👍

In your revision of this chapter, ensure that you are able to:

★ explain the need for stating the purpose of software before it is developed

★ explain the need for defining the scope and boundaries of software before it is developed

★ describe what is meant by the inputs, outputs and process of software

★ develop a full project specification from a given scenario.

Questions ❓

1 The developer works closely with the client throughout the analysis stage. Describe how the employees of the music venue may be involved in defining the:
   - purpose
   - scope
   - boundaries
   - inputs, outputs and processes of the Music Venue app. (4)

2 Read the following partial project specification carefully and answer the questions below.

Table 2.2 Partial project specification

Analysis	
Purpose	The purpose of the program is to provide amateur bird-watchers with a method of recording the names of birds that visit their garden.
	Each time they spot a bird, the watcher will use a printed chart to identify a single letter of the alphabet that should be entered into the program. The program will store the full name of the bird along with the user's postcode and the date.
	The program will also allow the user to select a bird type after which it will display the number of times the bird has been spotted.
	The program should store all the data it collects in an external text file so that the results can be emailed to the national survey team who have commissioned the program.
Scope	Not required for this question.
Boundaries	The program will store the bird-spotting information within a text file.
	The information for each bird spot event will be:
	● the name of the bird (e.g. 'sparrow')
	● the user's postcode (e.g. 'KY12 4HQ')
	● the date of the spotting event (e.g. '27012019').
	The program will only store information on the 26 most common garden birds.
	When the user searches for a type of bird, the information displayed will be limited to the name of the bird and the number of times it has been spotted.
	The program will loop continuously, waiting for letters to be entered, until the user enters 9. The user will then be asked what bird they would like to search for. The program will end after the number of times that bird has appeared is displayed.

⇨

⇨

Table 2.2 (*continued*)

Functional requirements	Information for previous bird-spotting data will be stored in a text file.
	Each process identified will be written as a procedure or function.
	Inputs:
	• user's postcode
	• date
	• bird letter.
	Processes:
	• validate user's postcode
	• validate date
	• convert a bird letter into the bird's full name
	• write new bird data to the end of a text file
	• input all the bird-watching data from a text file
	• count the occurrences of a user's selected bird
	• display the occurrence of the selected bird.
	Outputs:
	• file line (birdName, postcode, date)
	• bird name
	• bird occurrence.

   a) State the client in the above project specification. (1)

   b) Explain why the program is limited to storing 26 different bird names. (2)

   c) A greenfinch was spotted by a user living at GA3 7HS on 29 March 2019. State how this input would look in the text file. (1)

   d) When the program is written, it is tested with the following birds entered as input:

     a t z t e g a g 9. State the purpose of the 9 at the end of the input. (1)

3 Create a complete project specification for the following problem:

Guitar players tune each of the six strings of their guitar to produce a different musical note. Standard tuning is: E, A, D, G, B, E, with each letter (from A to G) indicating the musical note

Figure 2.3 Tuning a guitar

in order from the bottom string to the top string. Notes may also be identified as sharp (for example C♯). Two alternative types of guitar tuning (where the six strings are tuned to different pitches from the standard tuning) are 'dropped' and 'open'. Figure 2.4 shows a few examples of alternative guitar tunings, including the note for each string.

⇨

⇨

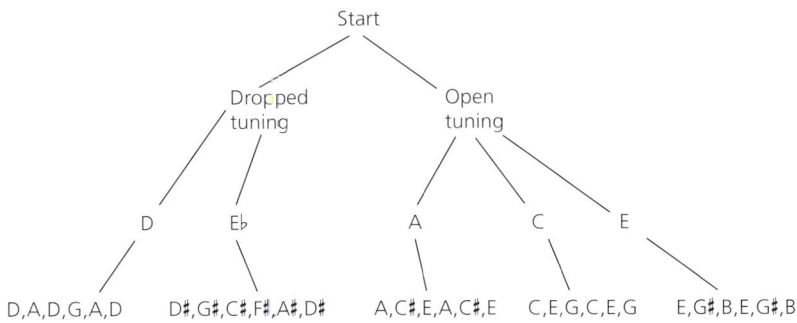

Figure 2.4 Alternative guitar tuning

A program is required that will ask the user for the guitar tuning they would like (for example, Open C). The program should then find and display the note for each string as shown below:

Open C tuning is:

Bottom string	C
2nd	E
3rd	G
4th	C
5th	E
Top string	G

Using the above information, create a complete project specification for the guitar-tuning program including:

- purpose (1)
- scope (1)
- boundaries (2)
- functional requirements (4).

## Chapter 3

Software design

Following the analysis of a problem, the software should now be designed. There are several aspects of design incorporated into the Higher Computing Science course including:

- identification of the main processes along with the data flow
- design of a programming solution using a top-down approach, which breaks the whole problem down into smaller and smaller sub-problems
- design of the user interface showing what any screens would look like
- identification of the types of data that will be stored (text, Boolean or numeric variables) and any structures that will be required to store multiple examples of related data (arrays or records).

Figure 3.1

Main algorithm

A software designer begins by identifying the main **algorithm**. This is the top level of the design showing just the main processes along with the data that flows in and out of each process. During your Higher course you will be expected to write, read and understand main algorithms written using both **pseudocode** and **structure diagrams**.

Data flow

The most common sequence of events found in programming is:

- input (take data in)
- processing (do something with the inputted data)
- output (store or display the result of the process).

Data flow identifies the data (and structures) being passed into and out of the main algorithm processes.

For example, a **module** (procedure or function) finds and returns the lowest score within 100 scores. This module would:

- be passed the 100 scores (input)
- find the lowest score within the 100 scores (processing)
- pass out the lowest score (output).

Figure 3.2 An example of data flow

If this were represented in pseudocode, the data flow in and out of the process would look like this:

```
Find lowest value within 100 scores (IN: scores(), OUT: lowest)
```

In both the assignment and exam paper you may be required to read and understand pseudocode with data flow. Here are a few points to note about data flow in pseudocode:

- An array is represented using empty brackets (). In the above example, 'scores()' is passed IN to the module.
- An array of records would be represented by including the record data inside the array brackets. For example, customers(forename, surname, accountNumber) would be an array called 'Customers' where each array element stores a single record made up of a forename, surname and account number for each customer.
- Single variables have no brackets. In the above example, 'lowest' is passed OUT of the module.
- IN and OUT are used to identify the data passed in and the data passed out of a module.
- It is possible for the same data to be passed in and out (IN: scores(), OUT: scores()). In this example we may assume that the module is altering the data in some way. For example, changing scores, deleting scores or adding more scores.
- It is possible for data to only be passed IN. For example, if the module were finding and displaying the lowest score there may be no need to pass the lowest value back out.
  Display the lowest score (IN: scores()).
- Data may be passed out of a process with no data passed in. For example, a module may ask the user for input which it then stores and passes out. Get survey information from user (OUT: surveys(name,address,rating)).

The Higher course requires that you can also read and understand data flow in structure diagrams. In this design methodology, a module is represented by a box and the data flow is represented by labelled arrows pointing in or out of the process.

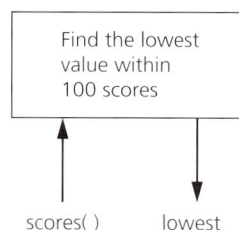

Figure 3.3 An example of a structure diagram

Whether written in pseudocode or represented as a structure diagram, the algorithm with data flow can be described as follows:

'An array of scores is passed into a module. The module finds the lowest value within the scores. The lowest value is then passed out of the module.'

A software design question in the exam may present a design using either pseudocode or structure diagrams. If you are asked to write a design, you will always have the option to use the methodology you are most comfortable with.

Example 1

A pseudocode design showing the main algorithm and data flow

The analysis of the Music Venue app in the previous chapter identified the purpose of the app and its main processes.

The main algorithm for this program may look like this:

1 Initialise data types and structures.
2 If required, add a new concert to a .csv file.
3 Read concert details from the .csv file (OUT: fileLines()).
4 Find a concert requested by the user (IN: fileLines(), OUT: concertTitle, startTime, setList(songTitle, duration)).
5 Calculate the finishing time of the concert (IN: startTime, setList(songTitle,duration), OUT: finishTime).
6 Display the concert set list and finishing time (IN: startTime, finishTime, setList(songTitle, duration)).

If this main algorithm was included in an exam question, what information could you extract from each step of the design?

- Although Step 2 is a module, it has no data passed in or out. The user enters the concert data and the module stores the concert information externally, in a .csv file. There will be no data passed back out of the module.
- Step 3 reads all the concert information from the external file. We know from our analysis that each concert will have the following information stored: concert title, number of songs, the song list (with times) and a start time for the concert. As the design shows one array being passed out of this process, we can assume that the information for each concert will not be split up at this stage. The array must simply store each line of text from the file as shown on page 14.

⇨

⇨

Index	'fileLines' array
0	Rock Warriors
1	10
2	Daydream City,00:03:45
3	Can't Remember You,00:04:10
4	Garden Colours,00:07:59
5	Head Banging Boy,00:02:26
6	The Longest Solo,00:10:03
7	Nights Ahoy,00:05:16
8	Trip to Japan,00:05:18
9	Funny Haha,00:01:40
10	Diary Moments,00:02:55
11	Home Time,00:07:00
12	19:30:00
13	The Blues Cirls
14	13
15	Closed Door Boogie,00:05:29
	…

- Step 4 of the main algorithm shows one array passed IN and multiple data types/structures being passed OUT. As the name suggests, the module finds the user's concert, stores the information and passes it out to be used later. The example below shows how the fileLines( ) array data might be copied into the two variables and array of records if the user's input was 'Rock Warriors'.

Index	IN: fileLines ( )		OUT: concertTitle, startTime, setList(songTitle,duration)
0	Rock Warriors		concertTitle
1	10		
2	Daydream City,00:03:45		
3	Can't Remember You,00:04:10		
4	Garden Colours,00:07:59		
5	Head Banging Boy,00:02:26		
6	The Longest Solo,00:10:03		
7	Nights Ahoy,00:05:16		setList(songTitle,duration)
8	Trip to Japan,00:05:18		
9	Funny Haha,00:01:40		
10	Diary Moments,00:02:55		
11	Home Time,00:07:00		
12	19:30:00		startTime
13	The Blues Girls		
14	13		
15	Closed Door Boogie,00:05:29		
	…		

⇨

⇨
- To calculate the finishing time of the concert in Step 5, the module requires the starting time (startTime) and the duration of each song (setList( )). The module passes OUT the calculated time: 'finishTime'.
- To display the required concert information in Step 6, 'startTime', 'finishTime' and 'setList( )' must all be passed IN to the final module.

Example 2 🏳

A structure diagram showing the main algorithm and data flow

The same Music Venue app example may be represented as a structure diagram showing the name of the program at the top with modules underneath. The order is important as it represents the order in which the processes will be carried out from left to right.

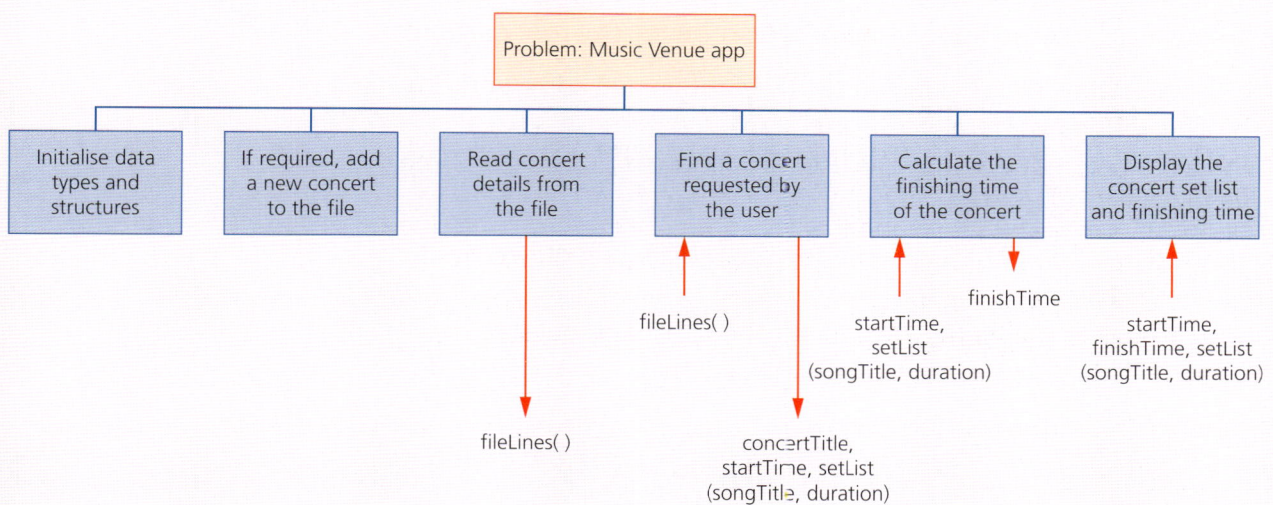

Figure 3.4 Another example of a structure diagram

By carefully reading the modules and data flow, the structure diagram can be analysed in exactly the same way as the pseudocode.

The importance of understanding the main algorithm and data flow

Learning to read the details written in the main algorithm and data flow is integral to understanding a problem. A good understanding of the steps required to solve a problem, and the data each step requires and produces, clarifies the purpose of the algorithm.

An ability to write, read and understand main algorithms and their data flow can also help a designer spot errors in their design. For example, the designs of the Music Venue app both show the 'concertTitle' being passed out of the 'Find a concert requested by the user' module. We can see from the remaining modules that 'concertTitle' is not being used by any other part of the program. There is therefore no need to pass it OUT of this process.

Refining steps of the main algorithm

Refining Step 4

After the main algorithm has been designed, the next stage is to look at refining each step of the algorithm. This involves taking each step in turn and describing how the processes in each step should be carried out. Once again this may be done using pseudocode or structure diagrams.

For example, below is Step 4 of the earlier Music Venue app algorithm (with concertTitle now removed from OUT).

4   Find a concert requested by the user (IN: fileLines(), OUT: startTime, setList(songTitle, duration)).

To refine Step 4, we will have to describe the processes required to:
- read in the fileLines array
- look through the array for the concert the user has requested
- copy the data found into startTime and setList.

A refinement of Step 4 is shown below:

```
4.1   Set counter to 0
4.2   Ask the user to enter the concert title they wish to find
4.3   Get requested concert from user
4.4   Start a fixed loop for each element of the fileLines() array
4.5      If the current element of fileLines() = requested concert
4.6         Copy the concert start time and set list data
4.7      End if
4.8      Increment the counter
4.9   End fixed loop
```

Note that when we refine an algorithm step, we number each refinement in a way that shows which step is being refined. Refinements of Step 4 become 4.1, 4.2, 4.3 and so on.

Further refinement of Step 4.6

Refinements may also need further refinements themselves. Step 4.6 states 'Copy the concert start time and set list data' but does not give any detail as to how this would be achieved. A further refinement may be:

```
4.6.1    Set songNumber to 0
4.6.2    Start a fixed loop2 from counter+2 to counter+2+number of songs + 1
4.6.3        Set setList(songNumber).songTitle to all the characters of
             fileLines(loop2) before the comma
4.6.4        Set setList(songNumber).duration to all the characters of
             fileLines(loop2) after the comma
4.6.5        Increment the songNumber
4.6.6    End fixed loop
4.6.7    Set startTime to fileLines(counter + 2 + number of songs)
```

The above is fairly complicated and probably beyond Higher in difficulty. When refining difficult solutions, you may find it useful to scribble ideas on paper as shown below. Note the numbering system for the further refinement of 4.6.

Table 3.1

Index	IN: fileLines ( )	OUT: startTime, setList(songTitle, duration)	Use of counter variable
0	Rock Warriors		counter = array index
1	10		counter + 1
2	Daydream City,00:03:45		counter + 2
3	Can't Remember You,00:04:10		
4	Garden Colours,00:07:59		
5	Head Banging Boy,00:02:26		
6	The Longest Solo,00:10:03		
7	Nights Ahoy,00:05:16	setList(songTitle,duration)	
8	Trip to Japan,00:05:18		
9	Funny Haha,00:01:40		
10	Diary Moments,00:02:55		
11	Home Time,00:07:00		counter + 2 + number of songs −1
12	19:30:00	startTime	counter + 2 + number of songs
13	The Blues Girls		
14	13		
15	Closed Door Boogie,00:05:29		
	. . .		

This may, of course, be just one solution to the problem of refining Step 4.6. Part of the skill of a software designer is the ability to create the most efficient design.

Refinements using structure diagrams

Similar refinements may be made to main algorithms expressed as a structure diagram.

Refinements start with the step to be refined written at the top. The problem is then refined using the structure diagram symbols introduced in National 5.

The same step previously refined in pseudocode is shown below as a structure diagram refinement.

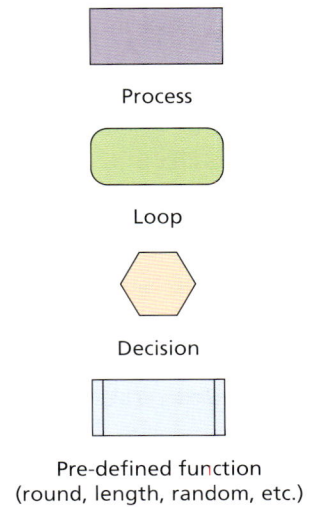

Process

Loop

Decision

Pre-defined function
(round, length, random, etc.)

Figure 3.5 Structure diagram symbols

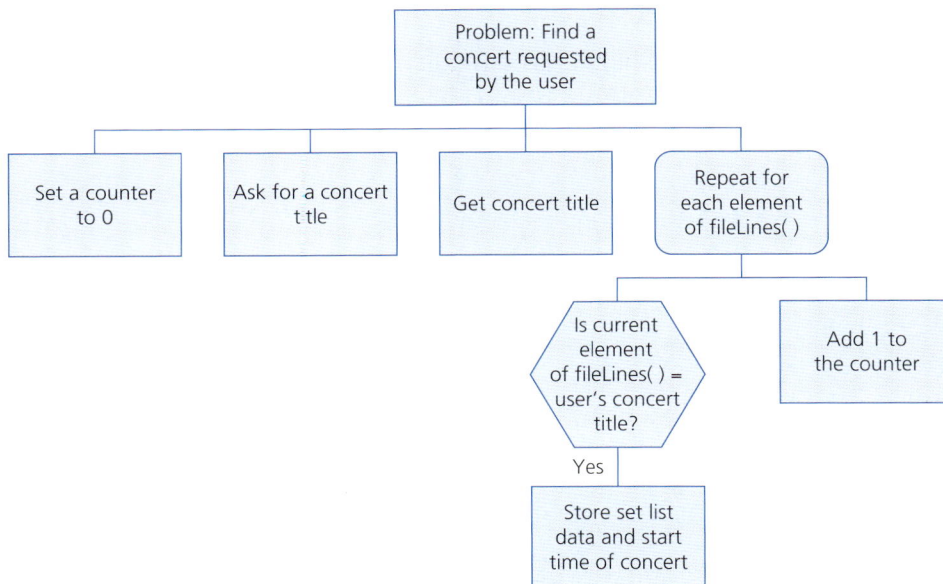

Problem: Find a concert requested by the user

Set a counter to 0

Ask for a concert title

Get concert title

Repeat for each element of fileLines( )

Is current element of fileLines( ) = user's concert title?

Add 1 to the counter

Yes

Store set list data and start time of concert

Figure 3.6 Refinement of 'Find a concert requested by the user' shown on a structure diagram

As before, part of this refinement may require further refinement.

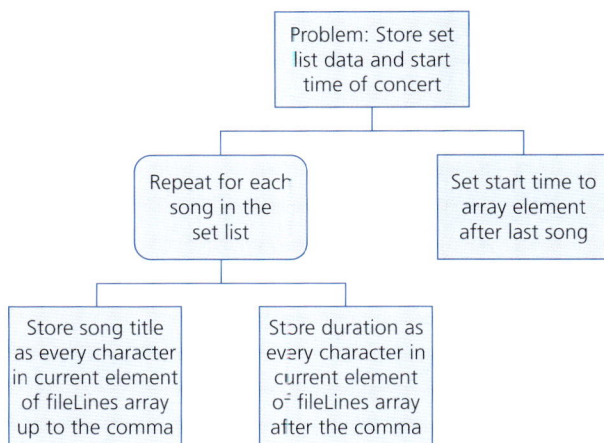

Problem: Store set list data and start time of concert

Repeat for each song in the set list

Set start time to array element after last song

Store song title as every character in current element of fileLines array up to the comma

Store duration as every character in current element of fileLines array after the comma

Figure 3.7 Further refinement

18

Some final points on designing programs

Notice that the previous pseudocode refinements define much more precisely how the 'Find a concert requested by the user' problem will be solved. The level of depth to which a problem solution is refined will depend on:

- company policy: there may be a house style that a designer must adhere to
- the experience of the programmer: a good programmer does not need the designer to refine a problem solution to a very high level of detail; this would be the software development equivalent of telling a professional skier how to put their ski boots on.

An ability to refine a problem is closely linked to an understanding of programming constructs. The more you code and improve your programming skills, the easier you will find reading and writing algorithms, data flow and refinements.

User interface design

The **user interface** is the part of the program that the user sees. A user interface design should show:

- instructions given to the user
- inputs the user is expected to give (keyboard input or mouse input such as a button)
- outputs produced by the program.

The style of the user interface will depend heavily on the programming environment. If you are coding in a programming language that uses simple text instructions like Python, your user interface may reflect this.

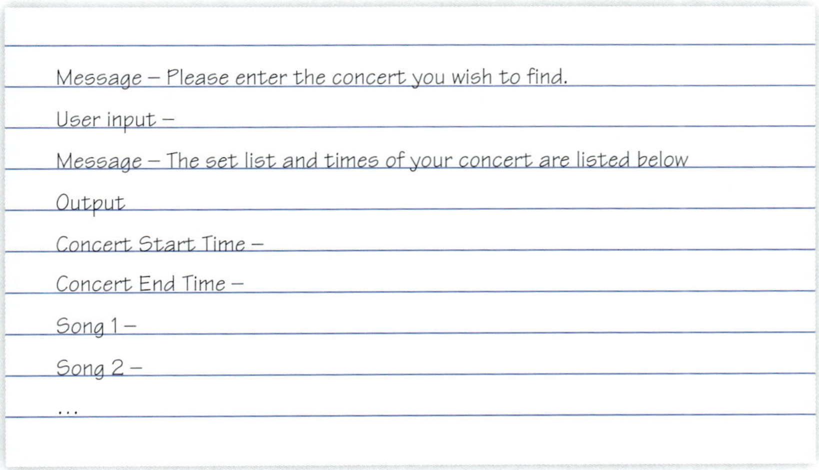

```
Message – Please enter the concert you wish to find.
User input –
Message – The set list and times of your concert are listed below
Output
Concert Start Time –
Concert End Time –
Song 1 –
Song 2 –
...
```

Figure 3.8 Text-based user interface design

If you are coding using an event-driven language like Visual Basic, then your user interface may contain graphics, text labels, buttons, input boxes and output windows.

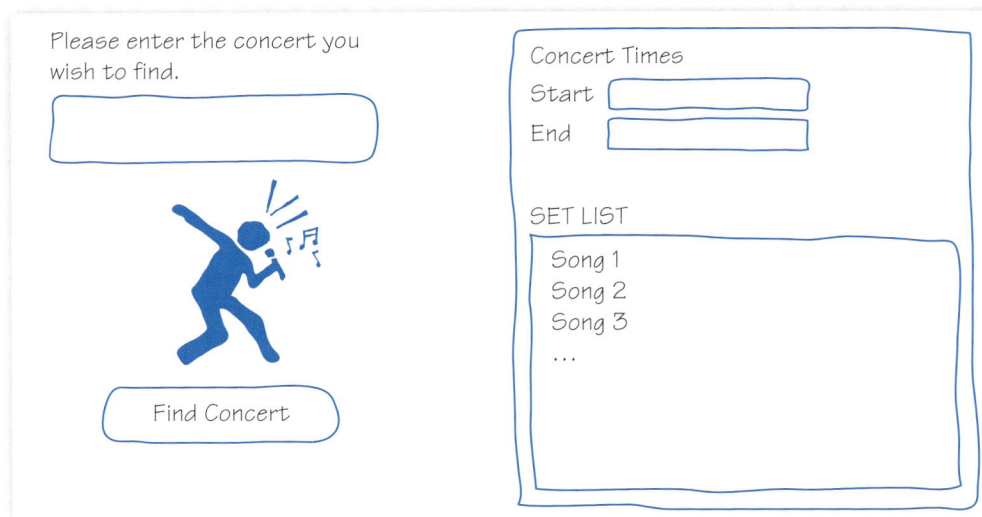

Figure 3.9 Graphical user interface design

What you should know

In your revision of this chapter, ensure that you are able to:

★ read, understand and explain a main algorithm design written in pseudocode or presented as a structure diagram
★ read, understand and explain data flow written in pseudocode or presented as a structure diagram
★ design a main algorithm, including data flow, from a given problem analysis
★ read, understand and explain refinements written in pseudocode or presented as a structure diagram
★ refine the steps of a given main algorithm using either pseudocode or structure diagram methodologies
★ from a given analysis, design the data types/structures required to store any input and output.

Questions

1 The analysis of the bird-watching problem (from the previous chapter) was used to design the main algorithm and data flow shown below:

1 Initialise data types and structures
2 Get user's postcode (OUT: postcode)
3 Enter and store bird spot events in a text file (IN: birdNames( ), postcode)
4 Read all bird details from the text file (OUT: birdData(name,postcode,date))
5 Find a bird requested by user (IN: birdData(name,postcode,date), (OUT: numberOfSightings)
6 Display the number of times the requested bird was spotted (IN: numberOfSightings))

a) Using the information in the analysis chapter as reference, describe all the data types and structures used above. (7)

⇨

b) Step 3 of the algorithm is refined as follows:

```
3.1    Open a write only connection to the text file
3.2    Start conditional loop
3.3        Ask user to enter a valid letter between a and z
3.4        Use letter to find matching bird name in birdName array
3.5        Ask the user to enter a valid date
3.6        Write bird name, postcode and date to a new line of the
           text file
3.7    End conditional loop when the user enters 9
3.8    Close the connection to the file
```

    (i) Explain why refinement 3.4 may itself require further refinement. (1)

    (ii) The refinement contains a conditional loop (3.2 to 3.7). Explain the purpose of this loop. (2)

    (iii) The final line closes the connection to the text file. Explain why the connection is closed in Step 3 even though Step 4 of the main algorithm requires access to the file again. (1)

c) Following feedback from the client, the main algorithm is redesigned. Rather than displaying the number of times the user's selected bird has been sighted, it should now also display the first and last dates the bird was sighted. Explain how the main algorithm would have to be changed to meet this new requirement. (2)

2 Step 2 of the Music Venue app is shown below:

```
2      If required, add a new concert to a .csv file
```

Using the example 'fileLines' array on page 14 for reference, refine Step 2 of the algorithm showing how the concert information would be input and stored. (5)

3 The functional requirements for the guitar-tuning problem are shown below:

Inputs   tuningType (dropped or open)
               tuningPitch (A, C, etc.)

Processes Get requested alternative tuning from user
               Find selected tuning in array of records (type, pitch, strings)
               Record example ('dropped",DD,A,D,G,A,D')
               Display formatted output of tuning for each string

Outputs   type
               pitch
               strings

Using the functional requirements above, design a main algorithm, including data flow, for the guitar-tuning problem. (4)

4 The Guitar Tuning app displays an alternative guitar tuning selected by the user. Design a graphical user interface for the app that includes the appropriate input, output and user instructions. (3)

## Chapter 4

Software implementation

Programming from National 5 to Higher

Unless they are keen programmers, National 5 students will complete their programming tasks in class, complete their assignment, sit an exam and then stop programming. If you feel that you have lost some of the skills you learned in National 5, it is important that you are comfortable with the following aspects of programming before you start Higher:

- creating and using data types (integer, real, character, string, Boolean)
- creating and using arrays
- making decisions (complex IF statements using AND, OR and NOT)
- using conditional and unconditional loops
- using input validation to ensure only valid data is entered by the user.

Programming designs at Higher will be presented as both pseudocode and structure diagrams. It is advisable that any revision/practice you do focuses on implementing these methods of design. Note that flow charts, which you also learned at National 5, are not part of the Higher course.

New data structures for Higher

The National 5 course introduces the concept of storing data in:

- **variables**, which store a single value
  - character – a single letter
  - string – a group of characters
  - integer – a whole number
  - real – a decimal number
  - Boolean – a true or false value
- **arrays**, which store multiple values of the same type.

There are many more data structures that are used by professional programmers. Three of these are introduced at Higher.

Parallel arrays

Parallel arrays are two or more arrays that hold related data within the same index value. For example, three arrays could be created to store the forename, surname and age for each member of a club.

index	forename( )	surname( )	age( )
0	Tony	Romeo	42
1	Sarah	Button	32
2	Bob	Bucket	45
3	Aharon	Klein	19
4	Dave	Stott	30
5	Grażyna	Kowalski	51
6	Matt	Wright	22
...	...	...	...

The data for Bob Bucket, aged 45, is stored at index 2 in all three arrays. The three arrays are completely separate data structures, but they are being used in a way that provides a logical connection between the structures.

Records

A **record** is a data structure that holds multiple data items about one entity. Each field within a record may store different data types, as shown when a record is declared using SQA Reference Language (SQARL):

```
RECORD Member IS { STRING forename, STRING surname, INTEGER age }
```

The code below creates a single member record called 'member1' initially storing Bob Bucket's details:

```
DECLARE member1 INITIALLY Member("Bob","Bucket",45)
```

The individual fields of a record are accessed using **dot notation** 'record. field' (similar to naming a field within a table in an SQL statement).

For example:

```
SET member1.surname TO "Bucete"
```

or

```
IF member1.age >= 25 THEN
    SEND member1.forename & "can apply for a bus driver licence" TO DISPLAY
END IF
```

Arrays of records

It is common to use multiple records within a program. An array of records stores single records within each element of an array.

index	clubMembers( )
0	"Tony","Romeo",42
1	"Sarah","Button",32
2	"Bob","Bucket",45
3	"Aharon","Klein",19
4	"Dave","Stott",30
5	"Grażyna","Kowalski",51
6	"Matt","Wright",22
...	...

How to declare an array of records is a common Higher exam question. In SQARL this is achieved using two lines of code.

First declare the record structure as before:

```
RECORD Member IS { STRING forename, STRING surname, INTEGER age }
```

Then declare an array of the record structures:

```
DECLARE clubMembers AS ARRAY OF Member INITIALLY [ ]
```

To declare the array with multiple elements, some additional code is added to the end of the SQARL array declaration:

```
DECLARE clubMembers AS ARRAY OF Member INITIALLY [ ] * 100
```

To access the records and fields within the array, the dot notation (element.field) is used.

```
FOR counter FROM 0 TO 99 DO
     SEND clubMembers[counter].forename TO DISPLAY
     SEND clubMembers[counter].surname TO DISPLAY
     SEND clubMembers[counter].age TO DISPLAY
END FOR
```

Programming Higher data structures

In Scotland, SQA does not tell schools to use one particular programming language. Your own school/college will have selected a language to teach with. How programming languages implement data structures such as records and arrays will differ from language to language.

As part of your revision, make sure that you select a few clear examples of parallel arrays, records and arrays of records from programs you have completed in lessons. These should be kept in an organised way so that you may refer to them during your assignment and during your revision for the exam paper.

Additionally, you should practise coding each data structure. If you only have access to your programming language in lessons, then make time to attend the Computing department outwith your normal class time. If you are taught using a free language like Python, you could ask permission to download and install it at home.

Modular programming

At National 5 level you are required to write short sequential programs where a program runs in order from start to finish. At Higher level you are expected to structure your programs using **modular programming** techniques.

Modular programming splits your code into logical blocks which are 'called' to perform a specific task or calculation. All professional code is written using modular coding as it offers several significant advantages to programmers, like reusing modules in other programs.

Modular programming example

The simple program below asks the user to enter a set of 'weight' values. The program then calculates and displays the average of those weights.

The program is written in a National 5 sequential code and Higher modular code to demonstrate the different style of coding. (# equals a comment line.)

National 5: sequential program

```
# Declare variables and data structures
DECLARE numberOfWeights INITIALLY 0
DECLARE totalWeight INITIALLY 0.0
DECLARE averageWeight INITIALLY 0.0
DECLARE weights AS ARRAY OF REAL INITIALLY [ ]

# User enters weights
SEND "Please enter the number of weights you wish to store" TO DISPLAY
RECEIVE numberOfWeights FROM KEYBOARD
FOR counter FROM 0 TO numberOFWeights-1 DO
    RECEIVE weights[counter] FROM KEYBOARD
END FOR

# Total and average are calculated
FOR counter FROM 0 TO numberOFWeights-1 DO
    SET totalWeight TO totalWeight + weights[counter]
END FOR
SET averageWeight TO totalWeight/ numberOfWeights

# The average is displayed
SEND "The average weight is:" TO DISPLAY
SEND round(averageWeight,2) TO DISPLAY
```

Higher: modular program

```
# User enters weights
PROCEDURE populateArray(ARRAY OF REAL allWeights)
    DECLARE numberOfWeights INITIALLY 0
    SEND "Please enter the number of weights you wish to store" TO
    DISPLAY
    RECEIVE numberOfWeights FROM KEYBOARD
    FOR counter FROM 0 TO length(allWeights)-1 DO
        RECEIVE allWeights[counter] FROM KEYBOARD
    END FOR
END PROCEDURE

# Total and average are calculated
FUNCTION findAverage(ARRAY OF REAL allWeights) RETURNS REAL
    DECLARE totalWeight INITIALLY 0.0
    DECLARE average INITIALLY 0.0
    FOR counter FROM 0 TO length(allWeights)-1 DO
        SET totalWeight TO totalWeight + allWeights[counter]
    END FOR
    SET average TO totalWeight / length(allWeights)
    RETURN average
END FUNCTION

# The average is displayed
PROCEDURE displayAverage(REAL average)
    SEND "The average weight is:" TO DISPLAY
    SEND round(average,2) TO DISPLAY
END PROCEDURE

# main program
DECLARE averageWeight INITIALLY 0.0
DECLARE weights AS ARRAY OF REAL INITIALLY []
populateArray(weights)
SET averageWeight TO findAverage(weights)
displayAverage(averageWeight)
```

The next few pages use the above modular program to explain
some of the programming concepts covered in Higher Computing
Science.

Procedures and functions

Modular code begins by defining each module. A module may be either
a procedure or a function.

- A **procedure** is a block of code that performs a task or calculation.
- A **function** is a block of code that performs a task or calculation and
  then returns a single value.

The example program comprises two procedures and one function:
- PROCEDURE populateArray – This procedure adds each weight entered by the user to the weights array.
- FUNCTION findAverage – This function totals all the values in the weights array, calculates the average and then returns the average.
- PROCEDURE displayAverage – This displays the average weight rounded to a number of decimal places.

Underneath the procedures and function sits the 'main program'. The program itself is substantially shorter than the National 5 version as most of the code has been placed in the above modules. The main program is the first part of the code to be executed when the program is run.

The main program in the example declares two variables and then 'calls' the procedures and function in order. Note that a call often 'passes' values to the module:
- populateArray(weights) – This calls the 'populateArray' procedure passing the 'weights' array into the procedure.
- SET averageWeight TO findAverage(weights) – This calls the 'findAverage' function again passing the weights array. The returned value is assigned (stored) in the variable averageWeight.
- displayAverage(averageWeight) – This calls the 'displayAverage' procedure passing in the variable 'averageWeight'.

Parameters

Values passed into modules are called **parameters**.

When values are passed into a procedure or function, the values in the call are matched to the values listed in the procedure or function definition.

For example, the (weights) array in the populateArray call is matched to the (allWeights) array in the procedure definition.

```
Definition    PROCEDURE populateArray(ARRAY OF REAL allWeights)
Call     populateArray(weights)
```

Actual parameters

The parameters used in the call to a module are called **actual parameters**. These are the actual values that are passed into the procedure or function. The actual parameters may be in the form of constant values, single variables or arrays. The data types of actual parameters must match with the corresponding data types listed in the function definition.

In the example program, 'weights' and 'averageWeight' would be actual parameters.

Formal parameters

The parameters used in the module definition are **formal**. These temporary parameters exist only within the module. At Higher level it is enough to think of formal parameters as copies of the original passed values.

The use of actual and formal parameters allows modules to be reused without the need to rewrite code. This is because formal and actual parameters can have different names. For example, the function

```
FUNCTION findAverage(ARRAY OF REAL allValues) RETURNS REAL
```

will calculate and return the average of any array that is passed into it.

```
SET averageHoursOfSun TO findAverage(sunHours)
```

or

```
IF findAverage(scores) > 50 THEN
     SEND "You passed the course" TO DISPLAY
END IF
```

or

```
SEND "The average reading is"
& findAverage(sensorReadings) TO DISPLAY
```

Pre-defined functions

Some functions are built into a programming language. The code for each function is stored in an external file called a **module library**. When a pre-defined function is used, this external module is called and executed in exactly the same way as the findAverage function in the example program.

Below is a call to a pre-defined function called 'round' that passes two actual parameters (average and 2) to the function.

```
SEND round(average,2) TO DISPLAY
```

In addition to the pre-defined functions you learned in National 5 (random, round and length), there are a few more you should be able to code with at Higher. The code for these will be specific to your programming language. As part of your preparation for the assignment and exam paper, you should collate at least one example of each from the programs you have completed in lessons.

Table 4.1 Some pre-defined functions

Pre-defined function	Definition	SQARL example

Sub-string	Extracts one or more characters from a string	```DECLARE word INITIALLY "grape"```
		```SET x TO String.sub(word,2,4)```
		```SEND x TO DISPLAY```
		
		This would output 'ap'. A sub-string of grape from position 2 to 4 as shown below.
		
		Figure 4.1 An example of a sub-string

Convert from an ASCII value to a character	Takes in an ASCII value and returns the equivalent character, for example, ASCII 89 would be converted to Y	```DECLARE x INITIALLY String.toCode(89)```
		```SEND x TO DISPLAY```
		This would output 'Y', the character represented by 89 in ASCII.

Convert from a character to an ASCII value	Reverse of the above function	```DECLARE x INITIALLY Integer.fromCode("Y")```
		```SEND x TO DISPLAY```
		This would output 89.

Convert from a floating-point (real) number to an integer	Removes the decimal places from a real number and stores the result as an integer	```DECLARE x INITIALLY 55.78```
		```DECLARE y INITIALLY Real.floor(x)```
		```SEND y TO DISPLAY```
		The pre-defined function 'Real.floor' removes the decimal place, effectively rounding the number down to the nearest integer. The output from the above would be 55.

Modulus	Divides one number by another and stores the remainder, for example 24/5 would store 4	```SEND 19 MOD 6 TO DISPLAY``` The output from the above would be 1 (6 divides into 19 three times leaving a remainder of 1).

Local and global variables

Variables may be declared within a procedure/function or as part of the main program. The variable scope diagram opposite shows where variables and arrays are declared within the average weight program.

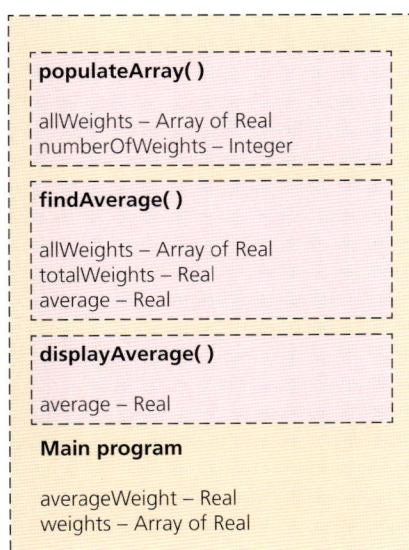

Figure 4.2 Variable scope diagram

Local variables

A **local variable** exists within a procedure or function. An example of this is 'totalWeight' found in the findAverage( ) function. This variable only exists while the function is being executed, and ceases to exist as soon as the program returns from the function to continue the main program.

If the line

```
SEND totalWeight TO DISPLAY
```

was added to the displayAverage( ) function, an error would occur when the program was executed, as within this function the variable totalWeight does not exist.

Local variables are vital in the development of larger programs. The array 'allWeights' exists locally in populateArray( ) and within findAverage( ). As these are both locally declared, they are completely separate data structures, despite being given the same name. Changing the contents of one will have no effect on the other. In large programs, the same variable names may be used within hundreds of different modules without causing errors.

Global variables

A **global variable** is declared within the main program. An example of a global variable in the program is 'averageWeight'.

A global variable can be used within any part of the main program or within any of the program's procedures and functions.

Care should be taken when using global variables in large programs as using the same global variable name twice would cause data to be overwritten, producing an error.

File handling

Programming languages often contain instructions used to access data held in external files. Without this functionality, all the data used by a program would have to be either stored in the code, entered by the user or received from an external device. The ability to use external files ensures that data can be:
- stored when the program is not running
- shared with other programs.

At Higher level, you are expected to write code that will read and write data to .txt and .csv files.

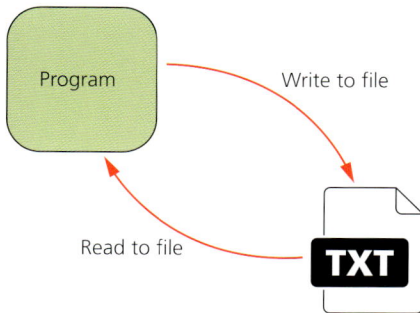

Figure 4.3 Read/write to external file

File handling examples using SQARL
Reading from a file

When reading from a file using SQARL, the entire file is read in a single string. This long string is then split up using the function split( ). This separates the lines (identified by the end of line character /n) and then splits the individual parts of each line (separated by commas). The example below uses a members.csv file.

fileText
Tony,Romeo,42/nSarah,Button,32/n Bob,Bucket,45/nAharon,Klein,19/n Dave,Stott,30/nGrażyna,Kowalski,5 1/nMatt,Wright,22/n

After split function		
[0]	[1]	[2]
Tony	Romeo	42
Sarah	Button	32
Bob	Bucket	45
Aharon	Klein	19
Dave	Stott	30
Grażyna	Kowalski	51
Matt	Wright	22

The example at the top of page 33 creates the array of Member records from earlier in this chapter. The file is opened, split and then each line is assigned to a new Member record in the array.

```
RECORD Member IS { STRING forename, STRING surname, INTEGER age }
DECLARE clubMembers AS ARRAY OF Member INITIALLY [ ]
OPEN "members.csv"
DECLARE fileText AS STRING INITIALLY "members.csv"
FOR EACH line FROM split(fileText,",") DO
    SET clubMembers TO clubMembers & [line[0],line[1],strToInt(line[2])]
END FOR EACH
CLOSE "members.csv"
```

The code required to read from a file varies depending on the programming language. As part of your revision you should find and collate a few examples from programs you have written in lessons.

Writing to a file

Writing to a file is fairly similar to reading from a file. The example below writes a list of US states and their populations, stored in parallel arrays, to a text file.

```
DECLARE stateList INITIALLY ["Florida","California","Texas"]
DECLARE population INITIALLY [20980000,39540000,28300000]
CREATE "states.txt"
FOR count FROM 0 TO length(statelist)-1 DO
    SEND stateList[count] & "," & population[count] & "/n" TO states
END FOR

CLOSE "states.txt"
```

Note that before a line is written to the file, it is formatted by concatenating a comma between the name of the state, the population and an end of line '/n'.

As before, you should find and collate a few examples of writing to files from your lessons.

What you should know 👍

In your revision of this chapter, ensure that you are able to:

★ write code, in a programming language of your choice, to:
  ★ create parallel arrays, records and arrays of records
  ★ create procedures and functions that pass parameters
  ★ create global and local variables
  ★ create .txt and .csv files
  ★ read/write data from/to .txt and .csv files
★ read and explain modular code written in SQARL
★ identify parameters within SQARL code and explain the difference between actual and formal parameters
★ identify local and global variables within an SQARL program
★ explain the purpose of modules and programs written in SQARL.

Questions ❓

1 Baycreal Community Hospital has been recording patient waiting times from when each patient arrives at Accident and Emergency to when they are seen by a nurse or doctor.
  The date and time (mins:seconds) of each patient's wait have been stored in a text file, formatted as shown below.

  …
  02/05/19,71:56
  02/05/19,74:16
  03/05/19,56:14
  03/05/19,68:20
  …

  ⇨

The following SQARL program is written to read in and analyse the waiting time data.

```
# Data is read from file
PROCEDURE populateArrays(ARRAY OF STRING dates, ARRAY OF INTEGER times)
    OPEN "waitingTimes.txt"
    DECLARE fileText AS STRING INITIALLY "waitingTimes.txt"
    FOR EACH line FROM split(fileText,",") DO
        SET dates TO dates & line[0]
        SET times TO times & convertToSeconds(line[1])
    END FOR EACH
    CLOSE "waitingTimes.txt"
END PROCEDURE

# Find the maximum waiting time
FUNCTION findMaxWaiting(ARRAY OF INTEGER times) RETURNS INTEGER
    DECLARE maxValue INITIALLY times [0]
    FOR counter FROM 1 TO length(times)-1 DO
        IF times[counter] > maxValue THEN
            SET maxValue TO times[counter]
        END IF
    END FOR
    RETURN maxValue
END FUNCTION

# Find the number of seconds when minutes removed
FUNCTION calculateSecs(INTEGER waitTime) RETURNS INTEGER
    DECLARE secs INITIALLY 0
    SET secs TO waitTime MOD 60
    RETURN secs
END FUNCTION

# Find the number of minutes in seconds
FUNCTION calculateMins(INTEGER waitTime, INTEGER secsWait) RETURNS
INTEGER
    DECLARE mins INITIALLY 0
    SET mins TO (waitTime — secsWait) / 60
    RETURN mins
END FUNCTION

# Display the longest waiting time
PROCEDURE displayLongest(INTEGER mins, INTEGER secs)
    SEND "The longest waiting time was:" TO DISPLAY
    SEND mins & " minutes" TO DISPLAY
    SEND secs & " seconds" TO DISPLAY
END PROCEDURE

#
PROCEDURE displayInfo(ARRAY OF STRING dates, ARRAY OF INTEGER times)
    DECLARE selectedDate AS STRING INITIALLY ""
    SEND "Enter a date" TO DISPLAY
    RECEIVE selectedDate FROM KEYBOARD
```

⇨

```
        SEND "Waiting times for selected date listed below:" TO DISPLAY
        FOR counter FROM 0 TO length(dates)-1 DO
            IF dates [counter] = selectedDate THEN
                SEND times [counter] TO DISPLAY
            END IF
        END FOR
    END PROCEDURE

    # Main program
    DECLARE waitingDates AS ARRAY OF STRING INITIALLY [ ]
    DECLARE waitingTimes AS ARRAY OF INTEGER INITIALLY [ ]
    DECLARE longestWait AS INTEGER INITIALLY 0
    DECLARE minsWait AS INTEGER INITIALLY 0
    DECLARE secsWait AS INTEGER INITIALLY 0
    populateArrays(waitingDates,waitingTimes)
    SET longestWait TO findMaxWaiting(waitingTimes)
    SET secsWait TO calculateSecs(longestWait)
    SET minsWait TO calculateMins(longestWait, secsWait)
    displayLongest(minsWait, secsWait)
    displayInfo(waitingDates,waitingTimes)
```

a) Identify all the global variables and arrays used in the above program. (2)
b) Describe the data structures waitingDates and waitingTimes in the main program. (2)
c) The populateArrays( ) procedure reads the waiting time data from a file. State the name and type of the file. (2)
d) Identify the following in the populateArrays procedure:
   ● every local variable (2)
   ● every formal parameter. (2)
e) A line within the populateArrays procedure calls the function 'convertToSeconds'. This function has not been included in the above code.
   Describe in detail what you think the purpose of the function convertToSeconds would be. (2)
f) The function calculateSecs( ) is called with the actual parameter longestWait. If the longestWait variable is storing the value 126 when calculateSecs() is called, state the values stored in the actual parameters
   ● secsWait
   ● minsWait
   when the displayLongest( ) procedure is called a couple of lines later. (2)
g) The comment line above the displayInfo() procedure has been left blank. Write a comment that would summarise the purpose of this procedure. (2)

2 State the difference between a procedure and a function. (1)
3 The text character '1' has an ASCII value of 49.
If '25' was read from a text file and stored as a string, describe how a knowledge of sub-string and ASCII values could be used to convert string '25' into the integer 25. (4)
4 A talent agency represents 50 actors. Sample data for one actor is shown below.
name: Vic Mortimer
age: 49
equity member: True
In a programming language of your choice, create a suitable data structure to store the above information on all 50 actors. (7)

## Chapter 5

Standard algorithms

Programming involves solving problems by designing algorithms. These solutions are then implemented using a programming language. While some of these algorithms will be unique to a particular problem, others appear regularly in different programs; these are known as **standard algorithms**.

Once implemented in code, standard algorithms may be saved as modules. This saves time later as the code to be reused is already written and tested. A collection of prewritten modules is called a **library**.

The four standard algorithms covered in Higher Computing Science are discussed in turn below. Examples are given using the SQA's Reference Language. This is the language that will be used in exam questions where you are asked to read and understand code.

Find maximum

The following **find maximum** algorithm finds the largest number in a list of values stored in an array. The algorithm compares each number in the array with the value stored in maxValue, and replaces the value stored in maxValue if a subsequent number is found to be greater.

```
DECLARE numbers INITIALLY [1,56,3,54,26,83,1,5,90,2,5]
DECLARE maxValue INITIALLY raceTimes[0]
FOR counter FROM 1 TO length(raceTimes)-1 DO
    IF raceTimes[counter] > maxValue THEN
        SET maxValue TO raceTimes[counter]
    END IF
END FOR
SEND ["The maximum race time was " & maxValue] TO DISPLAY
```

Find minimum

The **find minimum** algorithm is almost identical to the find maximum algorithm. To find the smallest value in an array, you simply swap the 'greater than' symbol for a 'less than' symbol.

```
DECLARE earthquakeReadings INITIALLY [3.4,6.3,2.9,7.6,5.5,1.8,4.2]
DECLARE minValue INITIALLY earthquakeReadings[0]
FOR counter FROM 1 TO length(earthquakeReadings)-1 DO
    IF earthquakeReadings[counter] < minValue THEN
        SET minValue TO earthquakeReadings[counter]
    END IF
END FOR
SEND ["The smallest magnitude earthquake was " & minValue] TO DISPLAY
```

Linear search

A **linear search** algorithm examines each value in an array, from first to last. This algorithm could be used to determine whether or not a value can be found in an array, or to search for and display specified values.

The example below examines a list of temperatures and displays each value that falls between 10 and 20 as it finds it.

```
DECLARE temperatures INITIALLY [9.65,4.77,12.89,19.99,10,23.33,34.26]
SEND "The values found are listed below:" TO DISPLAY
FOR counter FROM 0 TO length(temperatures)-1 DO
     IF temperatures [counter] >= 10 AND temperatures [counter] <= 20 THEN
          SEND temperatures [counter] TO DISPLAY
     END IF
END FOR
```

Count occurrences

A **count occurrences** algorithm displays the number of times that a value occurs in an array. This algorithm is based on the linear search algorithm in that both examine each element of the array.

The example counts the number of times a weight (in the weights() array) is between the values 15 and 18.

```
DECLARE weights INITIALLY [12,6,34,34,23,19,17,15,9,56,43]
DECLARE totalFound INITIALLY 0
FOR counter FROM 0 TO length(weights)-1 DO
     IF weights[counter] >= 15 AND weights[counter] <= 18 THEN
          SET totalFound TO totalFound + 1
     END IF
END FOR
SEND ["The number of weights found between 15 and 18 was " & totalFound]
TO DISPLAY
```

What you should know

In your revision of this chapter, ensure that you are able to:
★ read and explain standard algorithms written in SQARL
★ write code, in a programming language of your choice, required to implement each standard algorithm
★ read and understand minor modifications to each standard algorithm (for example, returning the position of the maximum value in an array rather than the maximum value itself).

Questions ?

1   Each of the standard algorithms (find max, find min, count occurrences
    and linear search) requires a repetition/loop to implement them. Explain
    why a loop is required in all four algorithms. (1)

2   In a programming language of your choice, write an additional procedure
    for the waiting-times program (Chapter 4, page 34) that will display the
    number of times a patient waited less than 1000 seconds. (6)

3   State the name of two procedures in the waiting-times program
    and the standard algorithm they use. (2)

4   Standard algorithms often have slight variations. In a programm ng
    language of your choice, rewrite the example 'find minimum' standard
    algorithm so that it finds, stores and displays the position (array index) of
    the minimum value in the array. (3)

## Chapter 6

Software testing

It is often thought that the purpose of testing is to see if a product works. In fact, the purpose of testing is to see that a product doesn't fail.

Testing a product once successfully shows that it works. To prove that the product doesn't fail, every possible thing that could go wrong must be tested.

Figure 6.1 Not all new products pass the test phase

Comprehensive program testing

When the product is a program, it should be tested comprehensively to ensure it meets the functional requirements identified during the analysis stage of development.

A comprehensive test may include some or all of the following:
- the program responds correctly to input
- each of the identified processes performs as expected including:
  - calculation results are correct
  - data is passed into the process and assigned without error
  - data is passed out or returned without error
- the program produces the required output
- the program reads/writes data correctly from/to external files
- the program processes data in an acceptable period of time
- the program has a usable interface
- the program runs correctly in its proper environment.

It is impossible to test most software fully as there may be an almost infinite number of possible inputs. A comprehensive test plan should document a systematic approach to finding as many possible faults in the software as is feasible.

Errors in program code

Testing aims to identify the following errors in program code in order to correct them:

- **Syntax errors** – Each programming language has its own set of rules regarding how the instructions must be written and formatted. If these rules are broken, a syntax error is created that will prevent the instruction being executed.
- **Execution errors** – These are errors that occur while the program is running. Execution errors, for example a division by 0, will crash a program.
- **Logic errors** – A logic error occurs when the code executes but produces the wrong result. Common errors may include AND instead of OR, < instead of >, code written in the wrong order, incorrect calculations or loops which repeat the wrong number of times.

Types and methods of testing

Testing may occur continually during the writing of a program by testing components such as individual procedures/functions, the integration of procedures/functions, interfaces and the final completed system. Several testing methods are included in the Higher course.

Dry run

A **dry run** is a form of testing that involves reading the program code and mentally 'walking through' it. The tester will predict what the code will produce and fix errors before the code is executed.

Trace table

Code is usually tested using a set of test data. This may involve the use of a **trace table**, which lists the program variables and tracks the values they store as the code is executed.

```
total = 0
for loop in range(1,10):
    number = int(input("Enter a value"))
    total = total + number
```

loop	number	total
1	4	4
2	8	12
3	2	14
4	5	19
5	7	26
6	9	35
7	2	37
8	5	42
9	4	46
10	7	53

Figure 6.2 A trace table

Breakpoint

A **breakpoint** forces executing code to pause at points defined by the programmer, allowing the current values of variables to be examined.

```
1 total = 0
2 for loop in range(1,10):
3     number = int(input("Enter a value"))
4     total = total + number
```

Variables

Name	Type	Value
{} globals	dict	{'_builtins_':{'ArithmeticError':
loop	int	2
number	int	4
pyscripter	module	<module 'pyscripter'>
total	int	4

The editor used to write the above code allows the programmer to add a breakpoint and then examine the current values of the program's variables.

Figure 6.3 A breakpoint

Watchpoint

To track events within a program, testers often add **watchpoints**. A watchpoint stops the program executing when a condition is met (for example, IF itemsInStock < 0) or when a variable changes value.

Both breakpoints and watchpoints may be used to check the current values stored by a program against expected values.

What you should know 👍

In your revision of this chapter, ensure that you are able to:

★ explain why comprehensive testing of software is required
★ describe different means of testing software
★ create a trace table for a given program and inputs.

Questions ❓

1   Identify the types of error that may occur from the program code and/or descriptions below:
    a) Code is mistakenly written using a minus sign instead of a plus in a calculation. (1)
    b) The line of code

```
SET result TO calcPercentage(readings())
```

   includes a call to a function defined as calculatePercentage (ARRAY OF REAL sensorReadings). (1)
    c) (1)

```
DECLARE start AS REAL 7635.85
RECEIVE end FROM INTEGER KEYBOARD
SET final TO start/end
```

2   For the code below, complete a trace table. (4)

```
Line 1   DECLARE x AS INTEGER 0
Line 2   DECLARE y AS INTEGER 2
Line 3   FOR loop FROM 1 TO 3 DO
Line 4      SET z TO x + y + loop
Line 5      SET x TO z
Line 6   END LOOP
```

3   When testing a program, it is suspected that a complicated calculation, carried out over several lines of code, is producing the wrong output.
    Describe how breakpoints may be used to find the possible error in the calculation. (2)

4   Every second, a program inputs readings from sensors and updates the values stored in three variables called sensor1, sensor2 and sensor3. Describe how the program could be tested to examine the values of sensor2 when sensor1 and sensor3 both store values greater than 100. (3)

5   Every good programmer reads their own code as they type and often catches errors before they run the code for the first time. State the type of testing being described by this behaviour. (1)

## Chapter 7

Software evaluation

To evaluate a software solution to a problem, the following should be considered:

Fitness for purpose

At the analysis stage, the functional requirements of a problem are identified. A program is said to be **fit for purpose** if it meets *all* of these requirements:

- reads in all the required inputs
- carries out the required processes
- correctly produces the required output.

Efficient use of coding constructs

As previously discussed, there may be many solutions to a problem, some of which are better than others. The solution should meet the requirements without unnecessary:

- lines of code (more code requires longer to process)
- repetition of code (code being used could often be placed within a module which is then called several times)
- use of variables and data structures.

Usability

The **usability** of a program depends on the clarity of:

- instructions given to the user
- error messages when something goes wrong, for example invalid input is entered
- formatted output, including messages/labels.

Maintainability

A program solution is **maintainable** if it can be updated easily in the future. A maintainable program will include:

- comment lines explaining the purpose of the code
- readable code that uses white space, indentation and meaningful variable/data structure names
- modularised code. The use of local variables and formal parameters in modules means changes to the main program are less likely to have any undesired consequences.

Robustness

A program is said to be **robust** if it runs without crashing. Robust code will validate inputs and be written in a way that anticipates possible run-time errors. For example, the addition of the IF statement below prevents a division by 0 error.

```
IF NOT(itemNumber = 0) THEN
    SET value TO cost/itemNumber
END IF
```

Assignment

Software evaluation involves the discussion of code compared to requirements. This is difficult to assess in an exam paper so it will more commonly be found as part of your assignment. Ensure that when you discuss the requirements listed on the next page you constantly make reference to your own solution. Stating 'my program is maintainable because I have used white space and indentation to make it readable by ensuring logical structures in the code stand out' will not be awarded marks if your actual code did not use white space or indentation.

What you should know

In your revision of this chapter, ensure that you are able to:

★ discuss solutions to problems in reference to:
  ★ fitness for purpose
  ★ efficiency
  ★ usability
  ★ maintainability
  ★ robustness.

Questions ?

Instead of answering questions on this chapter, you are advised to take solutions you have produced in class and practise writing evaluations on the code.

Area 2 Computer Systems

Chapter 8
Data representation

Two's complement

In the National 5 course you learned that integers are stored using simple binary numbers as shown below.

128	64	32	16	8	4	2	U	
1	1	1	0	1	1	0	1	= 128+64+32+8+4+1 = 237

Figure 8.1 Integers stored using simple binary numbers

This binary representation of integers only stores positive numbers. Storing negative numbers requires a different solution.

A common notation used to store negative integers is **two's complement**. In this method, the left-hand bit is used to store the negative equivalent of that column, while the remaining columns store positive numbers as before.

–128	64	32	16	8	4	2	U	
1	1	1	0	1	1	0	1	= –128+64+32+8+4+1 = –19

Figure 8.2 Negative integers stored using simple binary numbers

The largest negative value that can be stored using two's complement is when the left-hand (most significant) column stores a 1 and the remaining columns store 0s.

–128	64	32	16	8	4	2	U	
1	0	0	0	0	0	0	0	= –128

Figure 8.3 Largest negative number possible

The largest positive value that can be stored is when the left-hand column stores a 0 and the remaining columns store 1s.

–128	64	32	16	8	4	2	U	
0	1	1	1	1	1	1	1	= 64+32+16+8+4+2+1 = 127

Figure 8.4 Largest positive number possible

In the exam you may be asked to represent a number using two's complement. One method used to manually carry out the required conversion from denary to two's complement binary is shown below. In Higher you are required to represent binary numbers up to 16 bits in length.

Worked example ⚑

Two's complement representation

Using two's complement representation, show how the value −3160 would be stored as a 16-bit binary number.

Solution

Step 1: Begin by representing the positive equivalent (3160) of the number using 16 bits.

32768	16384	8192	4096	2048	1024	512	256	128	64	32	16	8	4	2	U
0	0	0	0	1	1	0	0	0	1	0	1	1	0	0	0

= 2048+1024+64+16+8 = 3160

Figure 8.5 Calculate the positive binary number

Step 2: Next, reverse all the bits in the number so that every 0 becomes a 1 and every 1 becomes a 0.

32768	16384	8192	4096	2048	1024	512	256	128	64	32	16	8	4	2	U
1	1	1	1	0	0	1	1	1	0	1	0	0	1	1	1

Figure 8.6 Flip the bits of the positive number

Step 3: Now add 1 to the right-hand units column using one of the following processes:

- If the column contains a 0, add 1 to the column = 0+1. As 0+1=1, a '1' is written in the column.
- If the column contains a 1: add 1 to the column = 1+1. As 1+1=2 (and we can't store a 2 in binary), the column is set back to 0 and a '1' is carried forward to the next column.

This above process is repeated for each column (moving from right to left) and will only stop when a 1 is not carried forward.

32768	16384	8192	4096	2048	1024	512	256	128	64	32	16	8	4	2	U
1	1	1	1	0	0	1	1	1	0	1	0	0+1	1+1	1+1	1+1
												1	0	0	0

1+1 = 0 (carry forward 1 to the next column)

Figure 8.7 Add 1 to the binary number

The final answer is written below. To ensure you haven't made any errors during your calculation, it is worth adding up the columns to check your answer.

−32768	16384	8192	4096	2048	1024	512	256	128	64	32	16	8	4	2	U
1	1	1	1	0	0	1	1	1	0	1	0	1	0	0	0

Check answer by adding columns = −32768+16384+8192+4096+512+256+128+32+8 = −3160

Figure 8.8 Two's complement answer

Floating point representation

There are many different representations used to store floating point numbers. SQA use a simplified version of the representation defined by the British Computer Society. In this representation:

- the number is stored using a total of 24 bits
- the mantissa is stored using signed bit representation
  - 1 bit is allocated to the sign (positive or negative)
  - 15 bits are allocated to the mantissa
- the exponent is stored using two's complement representation
  - 8 bits are allocated to the exponent.

As part of your Higher exam you may be asked to convert between a binary floating point number and the SQA floating point representation. To convert from binary to SQA floating point we work through the following steps:

- The decimal point is moved to the left of the most significant bit.
- The sign bit is set to 1 or 0: positive = 0, negative = 1.
- The binary number becomes the 15-bit mantissa. If there are any empty bits to the right of the number, these are filled with 0s.
- The number of places the decimal point moved is stored (using an 8-bit two's complement) as the exponent:
  - If the decimal point moved to the left, the exponent will be a positive number.
  - If the decimal point moved to the right, the exponent will be a negative number.

> **Worked example** 🚩
>
> ## A negative number with a positive exponent
>
> −11100.11101
>
> Most significant bit
>
> Move the decimal place to the left of the most significant bit.
>
> −.1110011101
>
> The sign is stored:
> 1 = negative
> 0 = positive
>
> The decimal point moved +5 places. This exponent is stored in two's complement.
>
> The binary number becomes the mantissa.
>
> | Sign | Mantissa (15 bits) | | | | | | | | | | | | | | | Exponent (8 bits) | | | | | | | |
> |---|---|---|---|---|---|---|---|---|---|---|---|---|---|---|---|---|---|---|---|---|---|---|---|
> | 1 | 1 | 1 | 1 | 0 | 0 | 1 | 1 | 1 | 0 | 1 | 0 | 0 | 0 | 0 | 0 | 0 | 0 | 0 | 0 | 0 | 1 | 0 | 1 |
>
> Zeros are added to the right of the binary number to complete the mantissa.
>
> ← 24 bit number stored →
>
> **Figure 8.9** Floating point representation: example 1

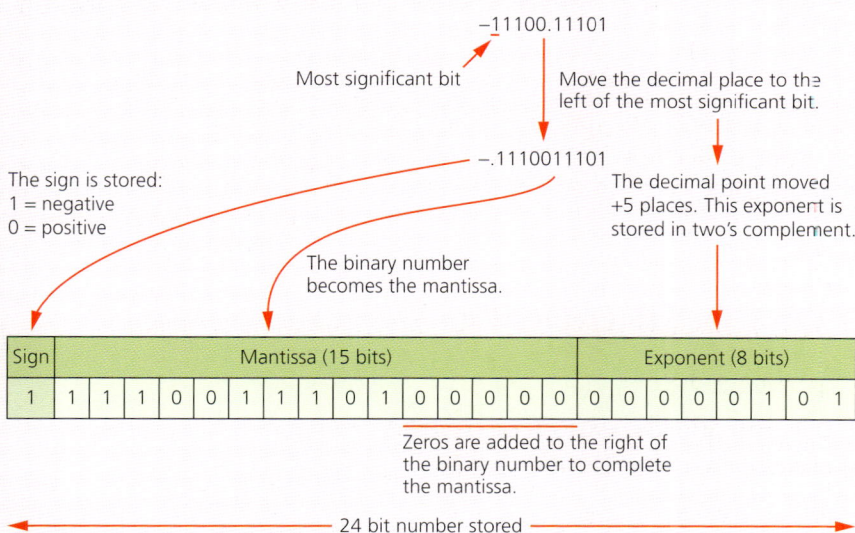

Worked example 🚩

A positive number with a negative exponent

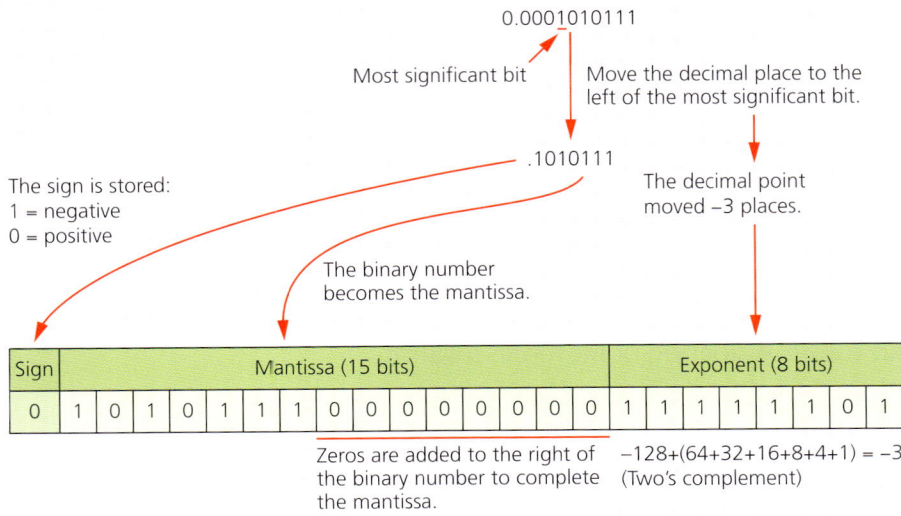

0.0001010111

Most significant bit

Move the decimal place to the left of the most significant bit.

.1010111

The sign is stored:
1 = negative
0 = positive

The decimal point moved −3 places.

The binary number becomes the mantissa.

Sign	Mantissa (15 bits)															Exponent (8 bits)							
0	1	0	1	0	1	1	1	0	0	0	0	0	0	0	0	1	1	1	1	1	1	0	1

Zeros are added to the right of the binary number to complete the mantissa.

−128+(64+32+16+8+4+1) = −3
(Two's complement)

Figure 8.10 Floating point representation: example 2

To convert a 24-bit SQA floating point number into a binary number, the process is simply reversed. Note that if the exponent is positive, the decimal point moves to the right; if negative, it moves to the left.

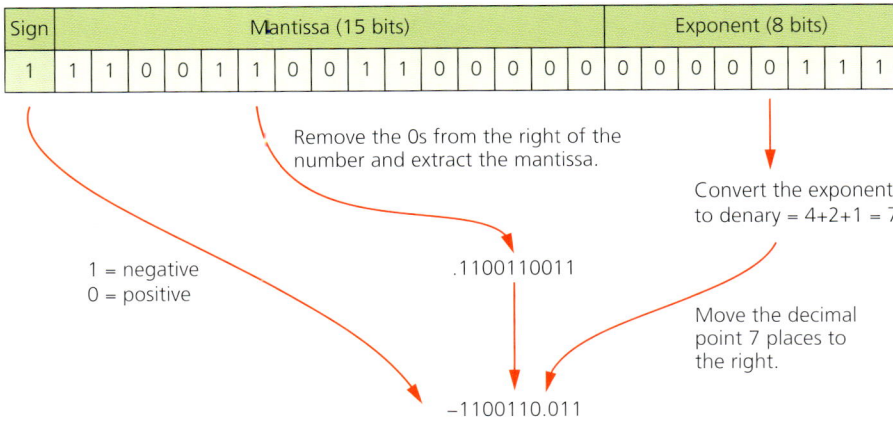

Sign	Mantissa (15 bits)															Exponent (8 bits)							
1	1	1	0	0	1	1	0	0	1	1	0	0	0	0	0	0	0	0	0	0	1	1	1

Remove the 0s from the right of the number and extract the mantissa.

Convert the exponent to denary = 4+2+1 = 7

1 = negative
0 = positive

.1100110011

Move the decimal point 7 places to the right.

−1100110.011

Figure 8.11 Floating point representation: example 3

Range and precision of floating point representation

The number of bits assigned to the mantissa and the exponent have an effect on the range and precision of the number that can be stored.

Precision

When storing the number 10110001000011110101.001101 using SQA representation, there are not enough bits to store the entire number in the mantissa.

10110001000011110101.001101

Move the decimal point.

.101100010000111`10101001101`

This part of the
number is lost.

Only the first 15 bits of
the mantissa are stored.

The decimal point
moved +20 places.

Sign	Mantissa (15 bits)															Exponent (8 bits)							
0	1	0	1	1	0	0	0	1	0	0	0	0	1	1	1	0	0	0	1	0	1	0	0

When we attempt to convert
back to the original binary
number, some of the initial
information has been lost.

.101100010000111

Move the decimal
point 20 places right.

101100010000111`00000.000000`

Lost information is
replaced with 0s.

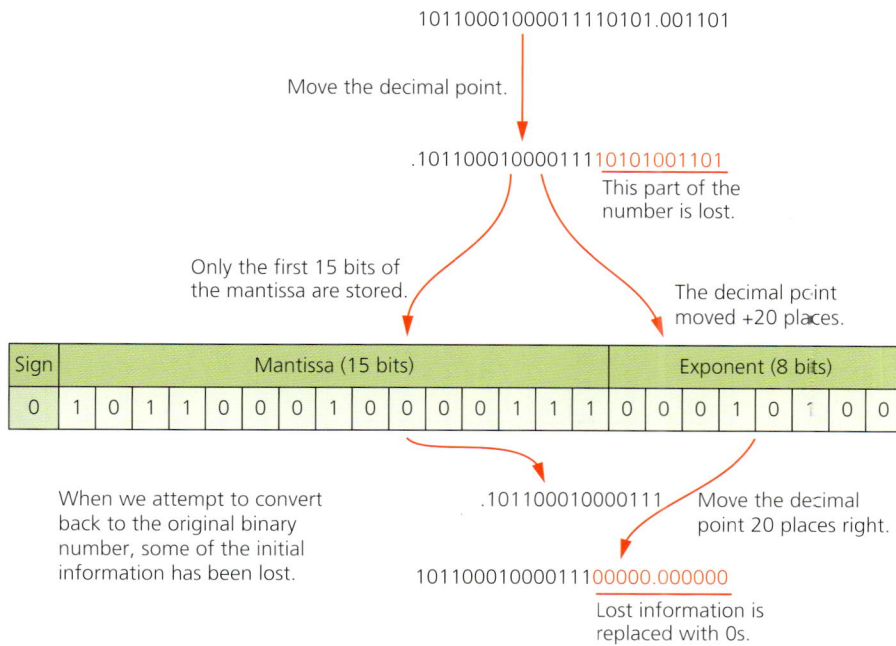

Figure 8.12 Floating point precision

The size of the mantissa limits how precisely the original number is stored. A larger mantissa would result in increased precision.

Range

The range, or smallest/largest number that can be stored, is determined by the size of the exponent. An 8-bit exponent can store the following values:
- smallest: −128
- largest: 127.

This means the decimal point can be moved 127 places to the left and 128 places to the right.

If the exponent was stored as a 16-bit number, it could instead store the following values:
- smallest: −32 768
- largest: 32 767.

Doubling the size of the exponent leads to the possibility of storing a significantly larger range of numbers.

Storing text (Unicode versus ASCII)

Text is stored by using a binary code to represent each character.

Extended ASCII is an 8-bit code used to store 256 different text characters. The ASCII code is limited to storing some control characters, numbers, the alphabet used in English and a selection of characters from other languages (for example, accents such as ú, ó, é).

Unicode is another code also used to store text characters. 16-bit Unicode can store 65 536 characters including many different alphabets, symbols and even emojis. Unicode is often used in web coding to display non-standard characters.

A sample of the type of data stored by ASCII and by Unicode is shown in Figure 8.13.

ASCII

6	00110110 (54)	W	00110111 (87)
7	00110111 (55)	X	00111000 (88)
8	00111000 (56)	Y	00111001 (89)
9	00111001 (57)	Z	00111010 (90)
:	00111010 (58)	[	00111011 (91)
;	00111011 (59)	/	00111100 (92)
<	00111100 (60)	]	00111101 (93)
–	00111101 (61)	^	00111110 (94)
>	00111110 (62)	_	00111111 (95)
?	00111111 (63)	`	00110000 (96)
@	00100000 (64)	a	00110001 (97)

Figure 8.13 ASCII and Unicode

Unicode

Greek and Coptic
Official Unicode Consortium code chart

	0	1	2	3	4	5	6	7	8	9	A	B	C	D	E	F
U+037x	Ͱ	ͱ	Ͳ	ͳ	ʹ	͵	Ͷ	ͷ			ͺ	ͻ	ͼ	ͽ	;	Ϳ
U+038x					΄	΅	Ά	·	Έ	Ή	Ί		Ό		Ύ	Ώ
U+039x	ΐ	Α	Β	Γ	Δ	Ε	Ζ	Η	Θ	Ι	Κ	Λ	Μ	Ν	Ξ	Ο
U+03Ax	Π	Ρ		Σ	Τ	Υ	Φ	Χ	Ψ	Ω	Ϊ	Ϋ	ά	έ	ή	ί
U+03Bx	ΰ	α	β	γ	δ	ε	ζ	η	θ	ι	κ	λ	μ	ν	ξ	ο
U+03Cx	π	ρ	ς	σ	τ	υ	φ	χ	ψ	ω	ϊ	ϋ	ό	ύ	ώ	Ϗ
U+03Dx	ϐ	ϑ	ϒ	ϓ	ϔ	ϕ	ϖ	ϗ	Ϙ	ϙ	Ϛ	ϛ	Ϝ	ϝ	Ϟ	ϟ
U+03Ex	Ϡ	ϡ	Ϣ	ϣ	Ϥ	ϥ	Ϧ	ϧ	Ϩ	ϩ	Ϫ	ϫ	Ϭ	ϭ	Ϯ	ϯ
U+03Fx	ϰ	ϱ	ϲ	ϳ	ϴ	ϵ	϶	Ϸ	ϸ	Ϲ	Ϻ	ϻ	ϼ	Ͻ	Ͼ	Ͽ

Storing graphics (vector versus bit-mapped)

Graphics may be stored as a **bit-mapped graphic** or as a **vector graphic**.

A bit-mapped graphic comprises rows and columns of coloured pixels. The storage requirements of a bit-mapped graphic are determined by the number of pixels (the resolution, for example, 1200 × 600) and the number of bits used to store each pixel (colour depth).

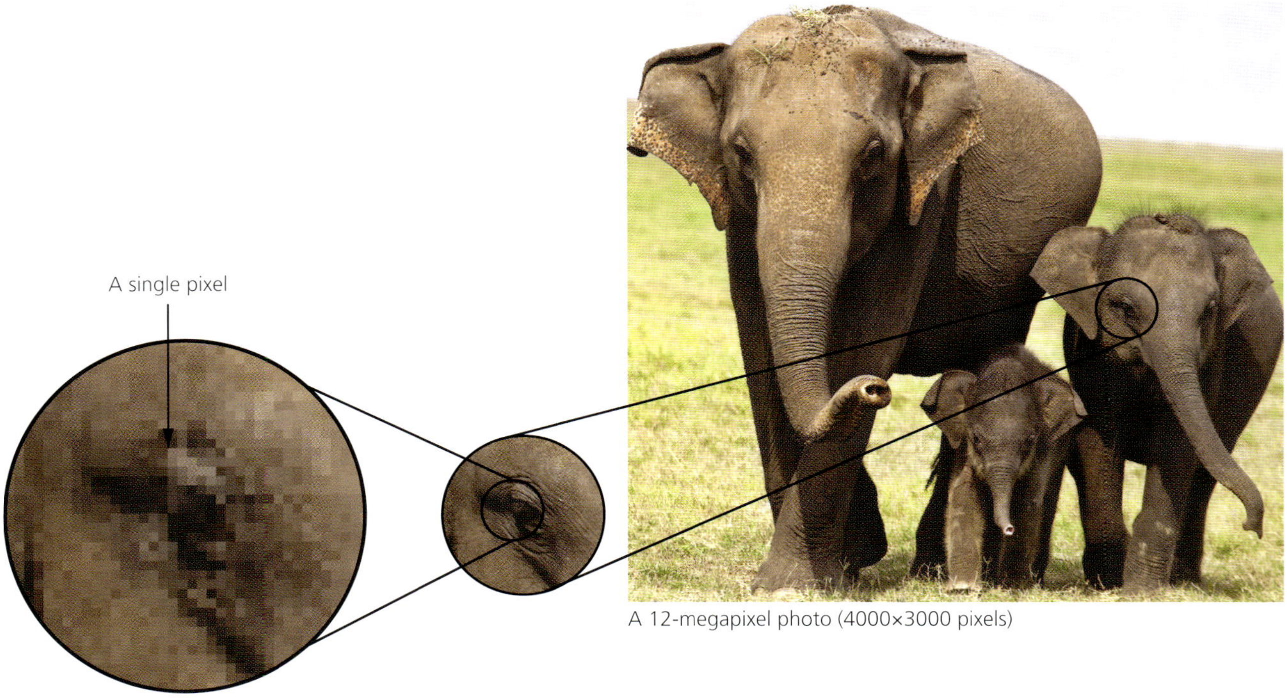

A single pixel

A 12-megapixel photo (4000×3000 pixels)

Figure 8.14 Bit-mapped graphic

A vector graphic is created from shapes, as shown in Figure 8.15.

Figure 8.15 Vector graphic

Regular shapes (polygons, ellipses, text) are stored by saving a list of attributes for the shape: x and y co-ordinates, length, width, fill colour, line thickness and so on.

Irregular shapes are stored by saving the position of nodes along with the angle the line leaves each node (determined by the position of the handles). The remaining attributes are stored as for a regular shape.

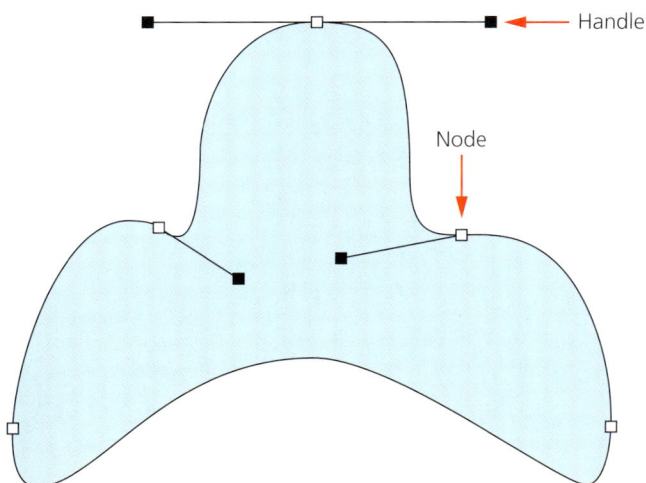

Figure 8.16 Vector graphic for an irregular shape

Table 8.1 compares the advantages and disadvantages of each graphic representation.

Table 8.1 Comparing the two methods of storing graphics

	Bit-mapped	Vector
Storage requirements	Storage requirements of bit-mapped graphics are determined by resolution and colour depth. A high-quality, digital photograph may require several megabytes of storage.	Storage requirements of a vector graphic are determined by the number and complexity of the shapes being stored. In most circumstances, a vector graphic will require less storage than a bit-mapped graphic.
Editing limitations	To edit a bit-mapped graphic, one pixel or a group of pixels are selected. The colour of the selected pixels is then changed.	A vector graphic is edited by altering the attributes of its shapes. It is impossible to change part of an attribute. For example, a single line can't be black with a small red section in the middle.
Layering	The pixels within a bit-mapped graphic cannot be layered as one pixel cannot be in front of or behind another.	A vector graphic stores a layer value for each shape. This is used to position the shape in front of or behind other shapes.
Resolution independence	If a low-resolution image is enlarged, the individual pixels become larger giving a blocky effect known as **pixilation** (see below). The resolution of a bit-mapped graphic cannot be increased without a loss of image quality. Bit-mapped graphics are called '**resolution dependent**'.	The resolution of a vector graphic is set by the resolution of the device that is drawing the graphic. If a vector graphic is enlarged on a monitor, the software displaying the graphic (browser, word processor, graphic editor, etc.) will redraw the graphic. Vector graphics do not pixilate when increased in size. Vector graphics are called '**resolution independent**'.
Displaying graphic representations	The four most frequently used bit-mapped file types are **bmp**, **jpg**, **gif** and **png**. These can be displayed by almost all software capable of displaying a graphic file.	To display a vector file type, software must be able to decode and draw the vector graphic. **Scalable vector graphic (svg)** is a common vector file type used to display logos, buttons, diagrams and cartoons.

What you should know 👍

In your revision of this chapter, ensure that you are able to:

★ convert a positive or negative denary number into an 8-bit or 16-bit two's complement number
★ convert a real binary into an SQA 24-bit floating point representation
★ explain how the number of bits assigned to the mantissa and exponent affects the range and precision of floating point numbers
★ explain the differences between ASCII and Unicode
★ describe the relative advantages and disadvantages of bit-mapped graphics versus vector graphics.

Questions ❓

1 Convert the following 8-bit two's complement binary numbers into denary.
   a) 0001 1111 (1)
   b) 1001 1011 (1)
   c) 0111 1111 (1)
   d) 1101 1111 (1)
2 Convert the following numbers into 8-bit two's complement.
   a) 122 (1)
   b) −121 (1)
   c) 91 (1)
   d) −12 (1)
3 Convert the following 16-bit two's complement binary numbers into denary.
   a) 1100 0010 1000 0011 (1)
   b) 1100 0000 0011 0110 (1)
4 Convert the following numbers into 16-bit two's complement.
   a) 24 161 (1)
   b) −31 505 (1)
5 Write the following numbers in SQA floating point representation.
   a) 1011.0101 (1)
   b) −111001.00110101 (1)
   c) 0.0010010110 (1)
   d) −0.0000110101011 (1)
6 If 24 bits used in SQA floating point representation were changed to:
   ◦ 1-bit sign
   ◦ 11-bit mantissa
   ◦ 12-bit exponent
   describe the effect this change would have on the range and precision of numbers that could be stored. (2)
7 State one advantage and one disadvantage of encoding text using Unicode rather than ASCII format. (2)

⇨

51

8 An editing application is used to overlap two digital photographs. Two images are then moved apart again, producing the image below.

Figure 8.17

State which type of graphics application was used to edit the photographs. Explain your answer. (2)

9 A vector graphic is drawn using a monitor set at a resolution of 120 dpi. State the resolution at which the graphic will be printed if the device is set to print at 800 dpi. Explain your answer. (2)

## Chapter 9

Computer structure

Although there have been significant developments in hardware complexity and processing speed, computer systems are still based on the architecture developed by mathematician John von Neumann in the 1940s.

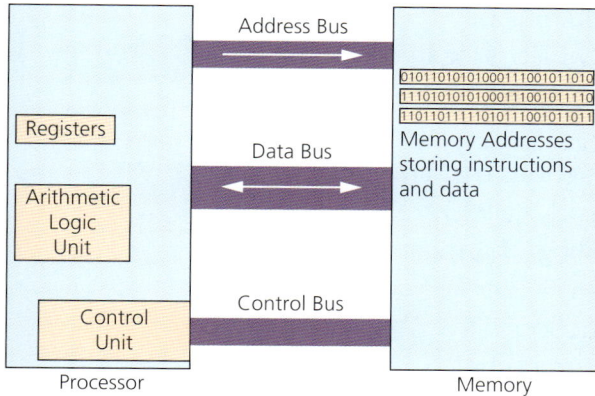

Figure 9.1 Computer system architecture

Fetch–execute cycle

While a program is running, buses are used to locate and then carry each program instruction from the memory to the processor where it is decoded and executed.

The **fetch–execute cycle** follows the steps below:
1 The memory address of the next instruction to be fetched is placed on the address bus.
2 The read line of the control bus is activated by the control unit.
3 The instruction is located at the memory address specified by the address bus. The contents of the address are then sent along the data bus to the processor.
4 The instruction is then decoded and executed by the processor.

Factors affecting computer system performance

Over several decades, solutions have been found to improve the processing performance of von Neumann computer systems.

Number of processors (cores)

Modern processors often have multiple cores, each capable of executing an instruction independently. Most programs run sequentially, requiring one instruction to be executed before the next, so new methods of programming had to be developed to take advantage of the 'parallel' processing capabilities of multicore processors where several instructions can be executed simultaneously.

Width of data bus

One simple way to improve a computer's performance is to increase the width of the data bus. If the data bus is widened from 32 bits wide to 64 bits wide, then twice the amount of data is transferred from the memory to the processor during each fetch–execute cycle.

Cache memory

Often the slowest step of the fetch–execute cycle is the fetching of instructions from memory. **Cache** is high-speed memory which is located near the processor. Cache uses the following techniques to speed up the fetch–execute cycle:

- Instructions that are regularly repeated (loops) or instructions that are frequently used (for example, a procedure that's frequently called) are retained within cache memory, while a program is running. This means that these instructions can be fetched much faster.
- The computer system doesn't wait until the next instruction in a program is fetched but rather preloads the instructions to cache, anticipating that they will be used next.
- If a processor wishes to store data temporarily, it will be faster to fetch the data again if it is stored temporarily in cache memory.
- The wide data buses (>=256 bits) found in cache memory mean more data is transferred in one cycle.

Clock speed

The clock within a computer system produces a pulse which other components use to time sequences of events, like the fetch–execute cycle. By increasing the speed of the clock's pulse (called '**over-clocking**'), a computer system may run faster, improving processing performance.

What you should know 👍

In your revision of this chapter, ensure that you are able to:

★ describe the four steps of the fetch–execute cycle
★ describe factors that affect a computer system's processing performance.

Questions ❓

1 Describe the role of the address and data buses in the fetch–execute cycle. (2)

The following are research questions designed to widen your understanding of this topic. You will not find the answers above.

2 To what does the term L2 often refer when associated with processors? (1)
3 State a possible catastrophic effect of over-clocking a processor. (1)
4 With which of the factors for improving system performance is the programming term 'threading' associated? (1)

## Chapter 10

Environmental impact

Computer systems are increasingly being used to save energy by controlling our environment. The Higher computing course lists three such systems.

Heating systems

Intelligent heating systems in large buildings collect data which allows the systems to make energy-saving decisions. Temperature information from sensors could also be used to control the heat of individual rooms by opening/closing windows or switching heaters on/off automatically.

Figure 10.1 These windows are opened and closed automatically to adjust the temperature inside

Modern heating systems may also:
- monitor activity within a building while making decisions to heat rooms only at certain times
- link to room-booking systems, allowing rooms to be heated just before use.

Within people's homes, central heating systems are increasingly being linked to the internet via the user's home wi-fi. Users can control their home-heating system from a remote location using an app, switching heating on for precisely when they will arrive home.

Figure 10.2 You can control your home heating using an app like this

Traffic control

Vehicles are at their most efficient when they are travelling at a constant speed. If they are accelerating, braking or sitting stationary in a queue of traffic, they produce even more carbon dioxide.

Traffic systems aim to keep traffic flowing, reducing traffic jams and thus reducing emissions. Through a series of sensors, cameras, traffic lights and electronic speed limit signs, traffic control software can make decisions that keep traffic moving.

Modern satellite navigation systems can warn the driver of potential congestion and suggest alternative routes.

Car management systems

The majority of modern cars are fitted with an engine management system. By processing thousands of readings each second from sensors, the engine management system can improve the efficiency of the engine, reducing the amount of carbon dioxide it produces.

Start/stop systems switch off a car engine when the car is stationary at traffic lights or during a traffic jam. Every second the engine is off rather than running, carbon dioxide emissions are reduced. When the driver pushes the accelerator to move forward, the car restarts automatically.

What you should know

In your revision of this chapter, ensure that you are able to describe how:

★ automatic heating systems help the environment
★ traffic control reduces congestion and therefore helps the environment
★ engine management systems reduce car emissions.

Questions

There are no questions in this chapter as exam questions will simply ask you to memorise and describe the above concepts within a new scenario.

## Chapter 11

Security risks and precautions

As computer networks grow and spread, so does the need to protect systems from attacks and prosecute those who access data illegally.

Computer Misuse Act

In 1990 the UK parliament created a law which is now used to prosecute people who do the following:

1. Gain unauthorised access to computer material. This could be either through hacking from a distance or gaining direct access to a computer.
2. Gain access with the intent to commit a further offence. For example, using the data/knowledge obtained to commit another crime like fraud or blackmail.
3. Modify data or programs on a computer system without authorisation.

Tracking cookies

Tracking cookies are small plain-text files that are stored within your browser when you access any website that uses cookies. When you return to a website, the stored cookie is sent to the server which responds by providing a personalised browsing experience.

Cookies may store the following data:

- Login details to log you back into a website automatically.
- Session details, for example retaining the contents of a shopping basket while you browse other pages within a website.
- Browsing behaviour, like websites you have visited or products you have looked at.

If this data is sent without encryption, a hacker could intercept sensitive data. Cookies should only be sent to sites using **HTTPS (Hypertext Transfer Protocol Secure)**.

Denial of Service (DOS) attacks

A **DOS attack** aims to prevent access to a computer system or network by legitimate users. This is usually achieved by flooding the system with meaningless requests. Attacks may involve:

- **Bandwith Consumption** – overloading the bandwidth of the network connection to the system
- **Resource Starvation** – causing so many processes to run simultaneously that systems become starved of resources (memory, processor time)
- **DNS Attack** – hampering access to a domain name server (DNS), the system that converts web address requests into IP addresses required to direct your internet connection to a requested website.

Symptoms of a DOS attack include an inability to access a system or experiencing extremely slow performance. For a company, this may result in lost revenue and unexpected costs required to resolve the attack.

DOS attacks may be carried out for personal, financial or political reasons.

Using encryption to secure data

Encryption is used to hide data from unauthorised individuals. Pairs of encryption keys – public and private – are used to scramble data so effectively that it cannot be read by anyone who intercepts it.

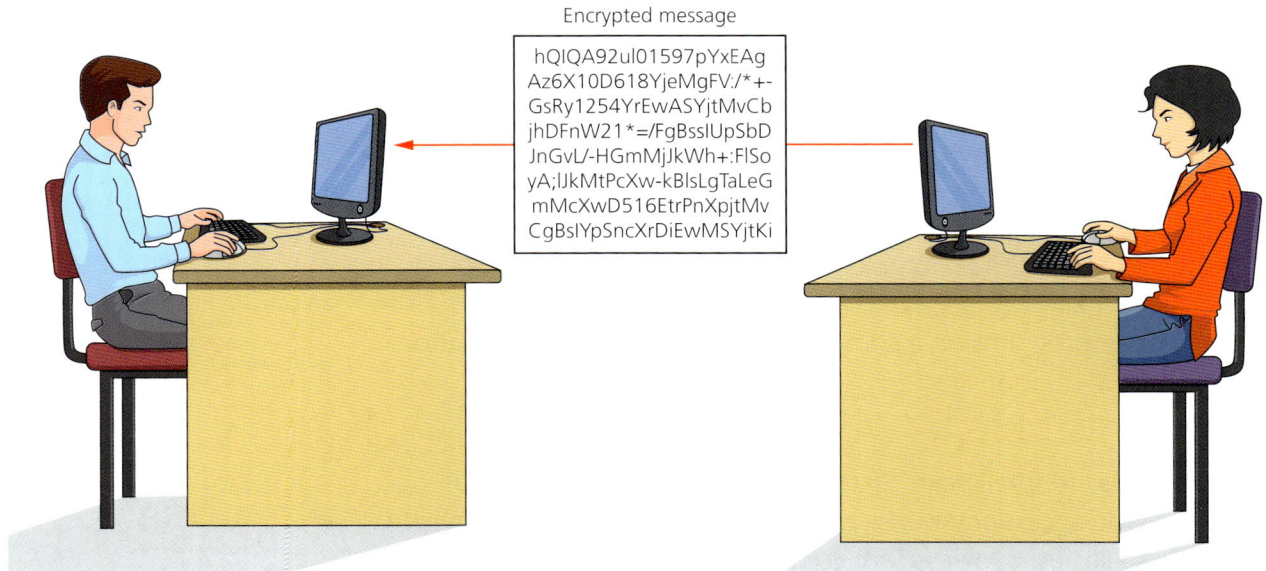

Encrypted message

hQIQA92ul01597pYxEAg
Az6X10D618YjeMgFV:/*+-
GsRy1254YrEwASYjtMvCb
jhDFnW21*=/FgBsslUpSbD
JnGvL/-HGmMjJkWh+:FlSo
yA;lJkMtPcXw-kBlsLgTaLeG
mMcXwD516EtrPnXpjtMv
CgBslYpSncXrDiEwMSYjtKi

Figure 11.1 The use of encryption keys

Rory has a pair of public and private keys. If Fiona wishes to send Rory a private message, she uses Rory's public key (available to everyone) to encrypt the message. When Rory receives the message, he uses the private key (which only he has) to decrypt the message.

Public keys are contained in a digital certificate, which acts as an online passport. A digital certificate contains the name, serial number, expiration date and **digital signature** of the authority that issued the certificate. **Digital certificates** are resistant to forgery.

What you should know 👍

In your revision of this chapter, ensure that you are able to:

★ state the principles of the Computer Misuse Act
★ explain the potential dangers of tracking cookies
★ explain the effects of a DOS attack
★ explain how data can be transmitted securely using public and private encryption keys
★ state definitions of the terms 'digital certificate' and 'digital signature'.

Questions ❓

1 Bethany receives an email offering her discounts on clothing she recently browsed on a well-known shopping website. State the type of file that Bethany may have on her computer system without her knowledge. (1)
2 A hacker writes a small program, which requests data from a targeted web server 100 000 times a second. State the type of security risk the website owner has failed to prevent occurring. (1)
3 Explain why public and private key encryption works only with pairs of keys. (1)
4 Explain how you could ensure that a public encryption key is authentic. (1)

## Chapter 12

Database analysis

Databases are structured stores of data. They are created either because a completely new system is required to store data or because of a need to computerise a system that currently exists. In both cases it is important to analyse the system that will be implemented.

The purpose of analysis is to identify the:
- **end-user requirements**
  - the people who will use the database
  - the tasks they wish to carry out with the database
- **functional requirements**
  - the information the database must store
  - the processes (searches, updates, etc.) the database has to carry out.

The Microsoft Access database used as an exemplar throughout these chapters, the community centre fitness class database, can be downloaded from the Hodder website: www.hoddereducation.co.uk/howtopass/higher-comp-sci. It may then be used to test SQL statements.

Worked example

Community centre fitness classes

A local community centre organises and runs several fitness classes every day of the week. During an interview with the centre staff, the following is discovered:
- Information about each individual class, the trainer who takes each class and a register of the community centre members who attend each class is all currently written in paper notebooks.
- Members are charged a fee for fitness classes.
- The fee varies depending on the type and duration of the class.
- The trainers are paid monthly.
- Their pay is calculated by multiplying their hourly rate by the total time of their classes.

The above information is used to identify the main entities in the system:
- a fitness class
- a trainer
- a community centre member.

The staff at the community centre are asked to write down the information they currently store on these entities.

$\Rightarrow$

⇨

Fitness Classes

- title
- level (beginner, intermediate, advanced)
- description of the class
- date and time
- duration of the class in minutes
- cost of the class
- number of fitness points
- name of the trainer who is taking the class
- names of members who take each class.

Trainers

- name
- address
- telephone number
- hourly rate of pay.

Members

- name
- address
- telephone number.

This is the minimum amount of information that must be stored to replicate the current paper-based system used by the centre staff.

The users of the database will be the community centre staff.

The staff will use the database to:

- keep the list of members up to date
- create new classes along with registers for each class
- keep the list of trainers up to date
- produce pay slips for each trainer at the start of each month
- produce a current fitness points total for centre members when requested
- produce lists of class dates and class times every week with descriptions of each class.

The completed database must be able to:

- insert/delete/update a member's details
- insert/delete/update a trainer's details
- insert/delete/update a class
- insert/delete/update a class register
- create a list of classes (trainer's name, title, time, duration, level, description) for a single day
- create a list of classes taken by a single trainer for a month along with the money earned for each class
- generate the total pay due to a trainer for one month's classes
- generate the total money paid by members for classes at the end of each day
- display a sorted list of the members' total fitness points
- display a list of the most expensive classes.

What you should know 👍

In your revision of this chapter, ensure that you are able to:

★ define what is meant by an end-user requirement
★ define what is meant by a functional requirement
★ identify a list of requirements from a description of a problem
★ identify end-user and functional requirements within a given problem analysis.

Questions ❓

Each of the phrases below appears in the worked example on pages 59–60. Find the phrase and identify whether this is an end-user requirement or a functional requirement.

1 'generate the total pay due to a trainer for one month's classes' (1)
2 'keep the list of members up to date' (1)
3 'number of fitness points' (1)
4 'insert/delete/update a class register' (1)
5 'cost of the class' (1)
6 'The users of the database will be the community centre staff.' (1)

## Chapter 13

Database design

The process of designing a database takes the requirements from the analysis stage and determines the entities, their attributes and the relationships between entities required to build the database. If the design stage is completed thoroughly, it should be a fairly simple process to then create the tables, fields and relationships that will become the finished database.

Entity occurrence diagrams

An **entity occurrence diagram (EOD)** collates real-life data and presents it as a simple diagram.

Worked example

Community centre fitness classes: entity occurrence diagrams

The relationship between fitness classes and members

Derek Boyle attends a spinning class and a yoga class every week. The yoga class is not only attended by Derek but also by Nayla, Aariz and Cary.

Data like this, along with many other examples, may be used to draw an EOD.

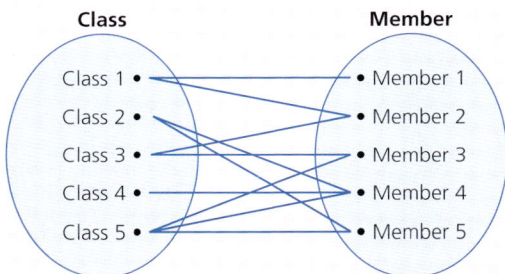

Figure 13.1 An entity occurrence diagram

Figure 13.1 shows that one Member entity can attend many Class entities and that a single Class entity can be attended by many Members. This is a **many-to-many (M-M) relationship**.

The relationship between trainers and fitness classes

The community centre only hires one trainer to take each class.

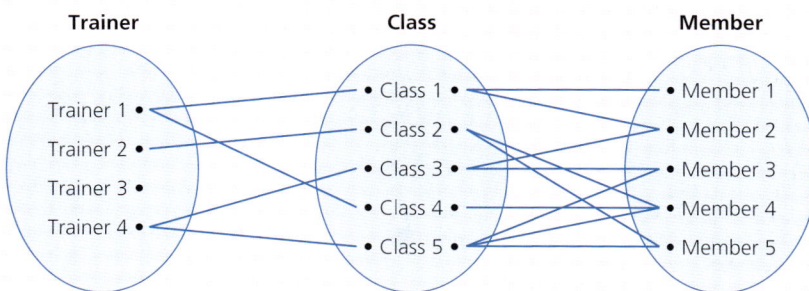

Figure 13.2 An entity occurrence diagram with the trainer

Figure 13.2 clearly shows that one Trainer entity can take many Class entities but a Class is only ever taken by one Trainer entity. This is a **many-to-one (M-1) relationship**.

Entity relationship diagrams

An **entity relationship diagram (ERD)** is used to show entities, attributes and the relationship between entities. An ERD is the first design stage where we begin to consider what will eventually become the tables in our database.

Worked example 🚩

Community centre fitness classes: entity relationship diagrams

The entities and their relationships have now been confirmed by analysing real data from the community centre. This can be represented in the basic ERD below.

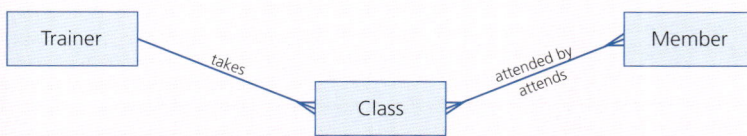

Figure 13.3 An entity relationship diagram showing entities, cardinality and relationships only

Figure 13.3 shows:

- three entities (Trainer, Class and Member)
- the relationships between the entities ('takes', 'attends' and 'attended by')
- the cardinality of the relationships (1-M and M-M).

The functional requirements identify the information that should be stored on each entity. These are its **attributes**.

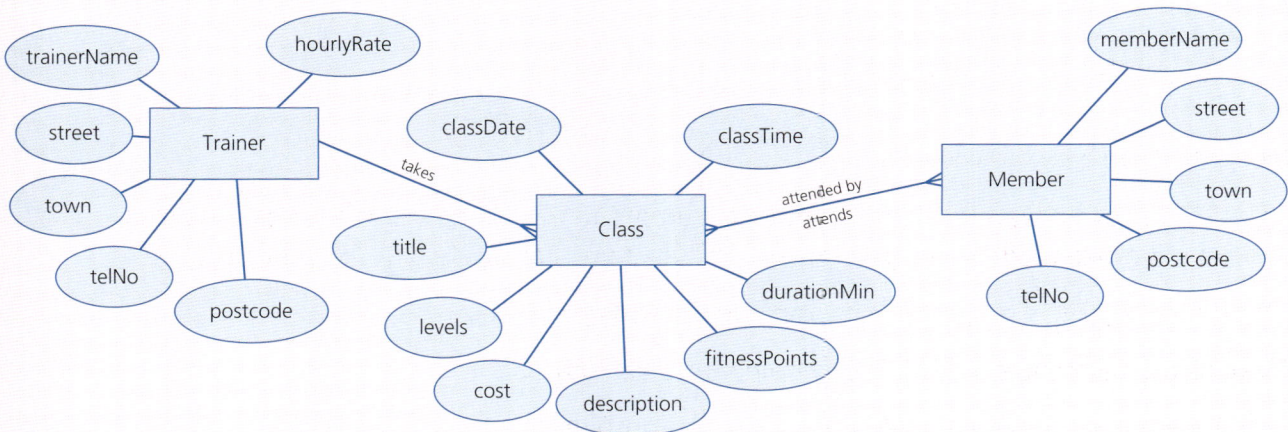

Figure 13.4 Entity relationship diagram showing attributes

Identifying primary keys and foreign keys

Each entity in the database must be uniquely identifiable. Unique attributes, or unique combinations of attributes, become a **primary key (PK)**. In an SQA entity relationship diagram, primary keys are <u>underlined</u>.

Where an entity doesn't already have a unique identifier, a new ID attribute is often added. This could be a membership number, stock code or a payroll number.

Where a relationship exists between entities, the primary key will be used to identify the link between the tables. The primary key is moved from one side of a relationship to the other side where it becomes a **foreign key (FK)**. In an SQA entity relationship diagram, foreign keys are noted with an asterisk (*).

Worked example 🚩

Community centre fitness classes: primary keys and foreign keys

Every entity in the community centre problem has no unique attribute. Each entity is therefore given a unique ID which becomes its primary key. Where a relationship exists between entities, a foreign key is also created.

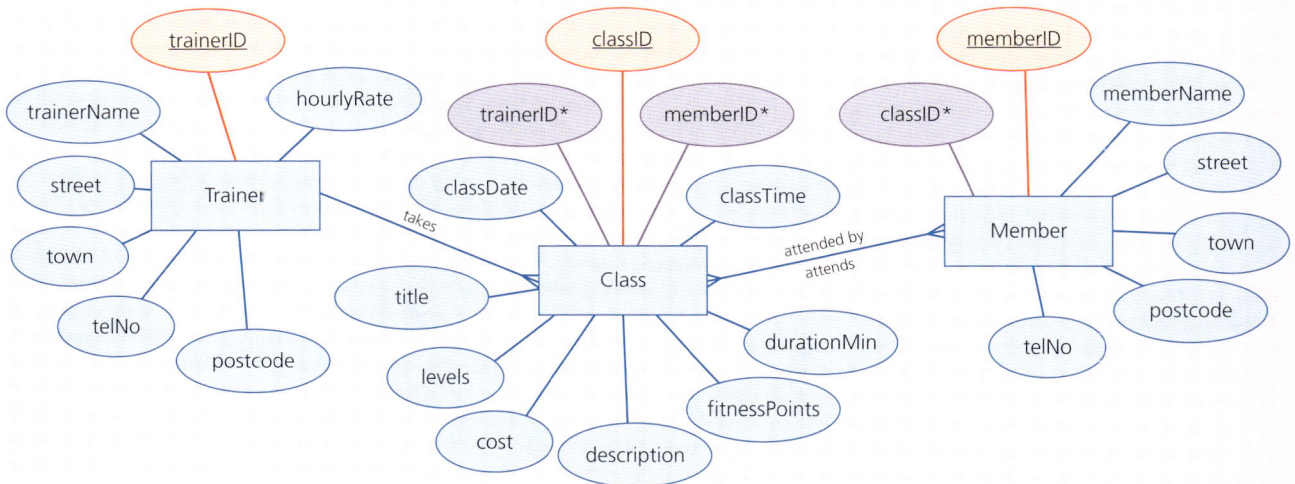

Figure 13.5 Entity relationship diagram showing primary and foreign keys

The M-M relationship is effectively two 1-M relationships, so a foreign key is created on both sides of the relationship.

Identifying repeating information

A good design should ensure that information is not repeatedly stored within the database. Where large amounts of information is duplicated, it may be necessary to create new entities.

Worked example ⚑

Community centre fitness classes: repeating information

Fitness classes take place regularly, with the same class being repeated on different dates and at different times.

The current design would result in the general information about each class being repeated.

Table 13.1

classID	trainer ID	class Date	class Time	title	levels	description	durationMin	fitness Points	cost
1	1	01/04/19	10:00	Zumba	Beginner	This is a …	30	5	5.00
2	1	03/04/19	12:00	Zumba	Beginner	This is a …	30	5	5.00
3	2	04/04/19	15:00	Zumba	Beginner	This is a …	30	5	5.00
4	1	08/04/19	10:00	Zumba	Beginner	This is a …	30	5	5.00

To ensure the highlighted information appears only once, a new entity is required. The highlighted attributes will be moved to this entity and a new PK created. We shall call the new entity 'ClassType'.

Table 13.2

Class				
classID	trainerID	classDate	classTime	typeID*
1	1	01/04/19	10:00	1
2	1	03/04/19	12:00	1
3	2	04/04/19	15:00	1
4	1	08/04/19	10:00	1

Table 13.3

ClassType						
typeID	title	levels	description	durationMin	fitnessPoints	cost
1	Zumba	Beginner	This is a …	30	5	5.00

The many-to-many relationship between Class and Member creates the same problem but this time in both entities. Within the Class entity, every member who attends a fitness class requires the Class information to be repeated. In the Member entity, the member's information is also repeated for each new fitness class.

Table 13.4

Class					
classID	trainerID	classDate	classTime	typeID*	memberID*
1	1	01/04/19	10:00	1	1
1	1	01/04/19	10:00	1	12
1	1	01/04/19	10:00	1	4
1	1	01/04/19	10:00	1	11

⇨

Table 13.5

Members						
classID*	memberID	memberName	street	town	postcode	telNo
1	1	Derek Boyle	12 Lance Dr	Redcorner	RE129HU	07865263464
12	1	Derek Boyle	12 Lance Dr	Redcorner	RE129HU	07865263464
35	1	Derek Boyle	12 Lance Dr	Redcorner	RE129HU	07865263464
36	1	Derek Boyle	12 Lance Dr	Redcorner	RE129HU	07865263464

Note that the primary key in each table is no longer unique so the above could not be implemented.

A simple solution to M-M relationships is to create a separate entity between the two tables as shown in Figure 13.6.

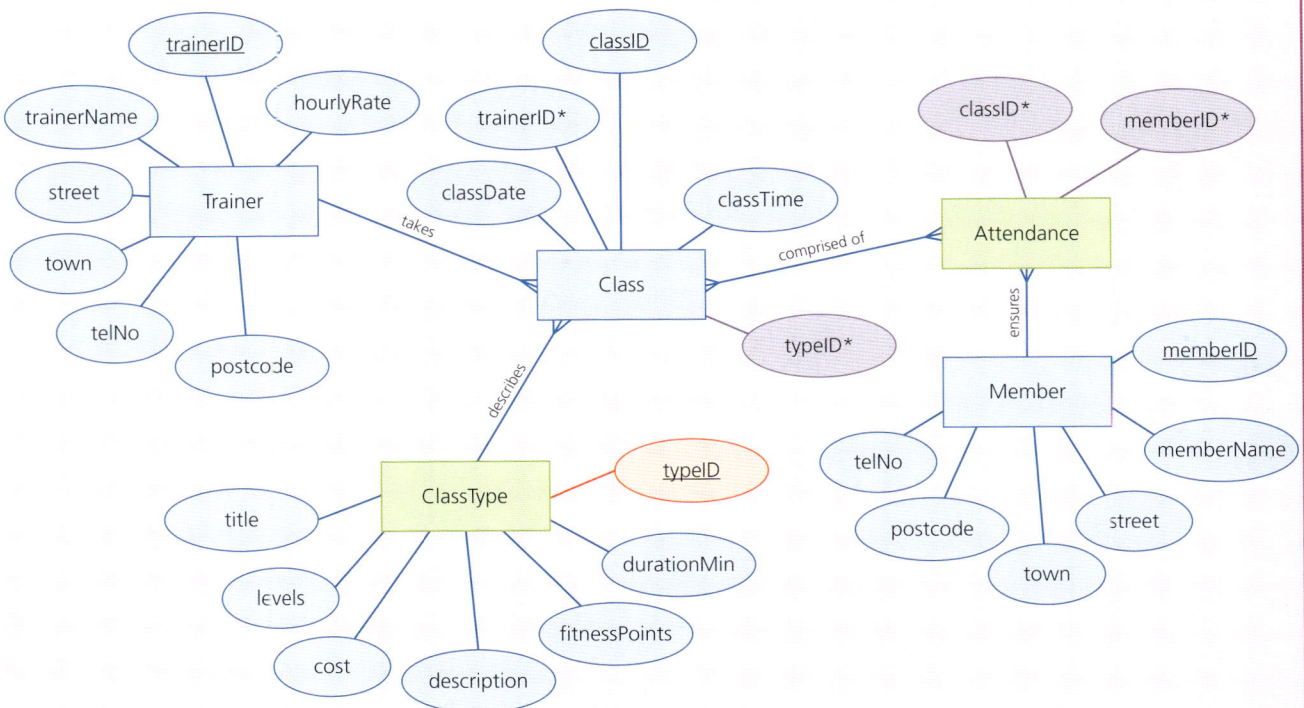

Figure 13.6 Entity relationship diagram showing new entities: ClassType and Attendance

The new entity includes the primary keys from each table, creating 1-M and M-1 relationships. This middle entity has been named 'Attendance' as it will store single instances of one member attending one class.

Compound keys

When two or more foreign keys combine to make a unique identifier (primary key), they are collectively known as a **compound key**.

Worked example

Community centre fitness classes: compound key

The two foreign key attributes in the Attendance entity are an example of a compound key. The combination of a single member attending a single class must be unique.

One-to-one relationships

A one-to-one relationship exists where one occurrence of an entity is related to no more than one occurrence of another entity.

For example, if a group of travelling sales people all had cars provided by their employer, this would be described as a **1-1 relationship**. Each sales person has exactly one company car. Each company car is driven by exactly one sales person.

Data dictionaries

A **data dictionary** provides precise detail about each attribute. The detail should be sufficient to implement the database. Data dictionaries were introduced in the National 5 course and remain unchanged in Higher.

If you are asked an exam question involving a data dictionary, the question will focus on Higher content, for example, identifying a compound key.

SQA data dictionaries are presented in the format shown in Table 13.6.

Table 13.6

Entity: ClassType					
Attribute name	**Key**	**Type**	**Size**	**Required**	**Validation**
typeID	PK	number		yes	
title		text	20	yes	
levels		text	12	yes	restricted choice: beginner, intermediate, advanced
description		text	255	yes	length >=30
durationMin		number		yes	range: >=30 and <=60
fitnessPoints		number		yes	range: >=5
cost		number		yes	
Entity: Attendance					
Attribute name	**Key**	**Type**	**Size**	**Required**	**Validation**
memberID	FK	number		yes	
classID	FK	number		yes	

Note that two attributes in the Attendance entity are both marked as foreign keys and there is no primary key. This suggests that memberID and classID together are a compound key.

Designing queries

In a Higher exam or practical assignment, you may be asked to design queries to:
- search for information (including grouping results or using wildcards to search for partial information in a field)

- sort information into order
- perform calculations (including the functions MIN, MAX, AVG, SUM, COUNT).

Design questions will usually provide data dictionaries, sample data or an ERD for a sample database as you need to be aware of the tables, fields, relationships and the format of stored information in a database before a query can be designed.

Sample information, including an alternative representation of the entities, attributes and keys, for the fitness class database is shown in the following tables.

Table 13.7 Fitness class database: tables and fields

Trainer	Class	ClassType	Attendance	Member
trainerID	classID	typeID	memberID*	memberID
trainerName	typeID*	title	classID*	memberName
street	trainerID*	levels		street
town	classDate	description		town
postcode	classTime	durationMin		postcode
hourlyRate		fitnessPoints		telNo
telNo		cost		

Table 13.8 Sample data for Trainer table

Table: Trainer						
trainerID	trainerName	street	town	postcode	hourlyRate	telNo
1	Kalem Logan	190 Christmas St	Alpfor	AL47DW	12.50	07936524345
2	Davey Jones	9 Water Drive	Sontisland	SN92SR	10.00	07772536478

Table 13.9 Sample data for Class table

Table: Class				
classID	typeID	trainerID	classDate	classTime
1	2	1	12/05/2019	12:30:00
2	1	1	12/05/2019	14:00:00
3	5	3	12/05/2019	14:00:00
4	4	2	13/05/2019	09:00:00
5	2	1	13/05/2019	10:00:00
6	2	3	13/05/2019	11:00:00

Table 13.10 Sample data for ClassType table

Table: ClassType						
typeID	title	levels	description	durationMin	fitnessPoints	cost
1	Zumba	Beginner	This is a Zumba class for beginners. The class will include two breaks to catch your breath.	30	5	4.50
2	Spinning	Beginner	An introduction to spinning. How best to use the bikes for maximum effectiveness.	30	5	3.00

Table 13.11 Sample data for Member table

Table: Member					
memberID	memberName	street	town	postcode	telNo
1	Derek Boyle	12 Lance Dr	Redcorner	RE129HU	07865263464
2	Josie Tarrent	1 Millenium Lane	Winner	HY84JN	07354274634
3	Cary Bryant	99 Dover Heights	Whitecliff	WE97NB	01418673464

Table 13.12 Sample data for Attendance table

Table: Attendance	
memberID	classID
1	1
2	1
3	1
5	1
3	2
4	2
6	2
7	2
7	3

Worked examples

Examples using sample data from the fitness class database

Example 1: Wildcards (% and _)

Design a query to display the names of all the members called Cary who have attended a class with a 'u' as the third letter of the title.

Table 13.13

	Answer
Field(s) and calculation(s)	memberName
Table(s) and query	Member, ClassType
Search criteria	memberName like "Cary%" title like = "_ _ u%"
Grouping	
Sort order	

Explanation of answer
- The 'memberName' field will be output.
- The query searches in, or displays information from, two tables: 'Member' and 'ClassType'.
- The memberName field stores both the forename and surname of each member so memberName = "Cary" would not work. The '%' wildcard is used to search for 'Cary' followed by any other characters '%'.
- The wildcard '_' can be used in place of a single character.
- '_ _ u%' means search for any title starting with any two characters '_ _', followed by the third character 'u', followed by any number of other characters '%'.

⇒
Example 2: COUNT occurrences (*), SORT

Design a query that will display the number of yoga classes that took place on each day. The output should be ordered from the most yoga classes per day to the least.

Table 13.14

	Answer
Field(s) and calculation(s)	classDate, Number of classes = COUNT(*)
Table(s) and query	Class, ClassType
Search criteria	title = "%yoga%"
Grouping	
Sort order	COUNT (*) descending

Explanation of answer

- The function COUNT(*) simply returns the number of rows in a table. A count can be grouped so that it counts the number of rows that have the same information, for example the same date. 'Number of classes =' shows that the results of the count will be given this alias when it is displayed.
- The search uses wildcards to include any mention of yoga in a title.
- The dates are sorted from the ones with the highest count to the least. To sort the actual dates into order this would be replaced by classDate (descending).

Example 3: SUM

Design a query that will display the total amount that member Dave White spent on fitness classes in 2019

Table 13.15

	Answer
Field(s) and calculation(s)	Member's name = memberName, Total spend = SUM(cost)
Table(s) and query	Member, ClassType, Class
Search criteria	memberName = "Dave White" classDate LIKE "%/2019"
Grouping	
Sort order	

Explanation of answer

- The query searches for Dave White and uses a wildcard to identify any date in 2019.
- The query will display Dave's name and will add up (SUM) all the costs from the ClassType table for those classes identified by the search.

Example 4: Calculations

Design a query to calculate how much trainerID 3 should be paid for the class they took on 8 March 2019.

⇒

⇒

Table 13.16

	Answer
Field(s) and calculation(s)	Trainer = trainerName, Payment = durationMin/60*hourlyRate
Table(s) and query	Trainer, Class, ClassType
Search criteria	Class.trainerID = 3 classDate = "08/03/2019"
Grouping	
Sort order	

Explanation of answer

- The calculation converts the fitness class duration to hours (/60) and then multiplies by the trainer's hourly rate.
- The trainerID appears in two tables, so the table may also be identified in the search criteria. This is called **dot notation**: Class.trainerID.

Example 5: Grouping

Design a query to count the total number of classes taken by each trainer and sort them from the trainer who has taken the most to the trainer who has taken the least number of classes.

Table 13.17

	Answer
Field(s) and calculation(s)	trainerID, COUNT(*)
Table(s) and query	Class
Search criteria	
Grouping	trainerID
Sort order	COUNT (*) descending

Explanation of answer

- When grouping is used, the table records that contain the same value are grouped together. If there are five different trainerIDs in the database, the output will contain five rows.
- Using the COUNT function displays the number of rows that meet the search criteria in the database. When combined with grouping, this displays a count of the number of occurrences in each group.

Using the results of one query in another query

Occasionally it requires more than one step to arrive at the correct output. For example, to find all the fitness class costs that were above the average cost of a class we have to:

1 calculate the average cost of classes
2 search for costs greater than that average.

Worked example ⚑

Example 6: Aggregate function followed by a calculation

Design a query to calculate the total wages for trainer 'Karen Gilly' from 1 January 2019 to 31 March 2019.

Table 13.18

Query 1	Answer
Field(s) and calculation(s)	totalMins = SUM(durationMin)
Table(s) and query	Trainer, Class, ClassType
Search criteria	trainerName = "Karen Gilly"
	classDate >= "01/01/2019"
	classDate <= "31/03/2019"
Grouping	
Sort order	

Table 13.19

Query 2	Answer
Field(s) and calculation(s)	Trainer = trainerName, totalMins/60*hourlyRate
Table(s) and query	Trainer, Query 1
Search criteria	trainerName = "Karen Gilly"
Grouping	
Sort order	

Explanation of answer

- Query 1 finds the total minutes worked by Karen Gilly between the given dates.
- The second query uses the field (totalMins) and table (Query 1) created by the first query to complete the calculation.

What you should know 👍

In your revision of this chapter, ensure that you are able to:

★ identify entities and their attributes
★ identify the types of relationship between entities
★ create, read and explain the purpose of entity occurrence diagrams
★ create, read and explain the purpose of entity relationship diagrams
★ write designs for queries using aliases, aggregate functions and calculations.

Questions ?

1 State one negative consequence of M-M relationships in relational databases and how are they avoided when designing a database? (2)

2 The following information is collected as part of an analysis of a plant nursery that sells young plants. Draw an entity occurrence diagram to represent this information. (1)

Table 13.20

SoilType	Category
soilType 1	category 1
soilType 2	category 3
soilType 4	category 1
soilType 3	category 2
soilType 5	category 4

PlantName	Category
plantName 1	category 3
plantName 4	category 2
plantName 3	category 2
plantName 2	category 3
plantName 5	category 3

3 State the relationships between SoilType, Category and PlantName. (2)

4 A garden centre sells products online to customers. The customer is required to enter their name, address, email address and telephone number. Customers can read a description of each item for sale along with the number of each item the garden centre currently have in stock. Once they complete an online order, the customer is sent a confirmation email with the details of their order including: an order number, the method of purchase and an expected delivery date. For each order, the garden centre stores the item code, item name and the quantity of each item.

Assuming that a single customer can place many orders and exactly the same order could be made by many customers, draw an ERD to design the entities and attributes required to store all the garden centre's information on their customers, orders and the number of items they have in stock. (7)

Questions 5 and 6 refer to the ERD given as the answer for question 4.

5 Explain how each OrderItem could be uniquely identified. (2)

6 Using the community centre fitness class database, (accessed from the Hodder Gibson website – see page 59), design queries to produce the following output.
  a) Display all the members (names and telephone numbers) with the surname 'Smith' who attended classID 35. (3)
  b) Display a list of the classes (title, duration and fitness points) being taken by the trainer Brian Clark, tomorrow morning (30/11/2019). Display the classes in descending order of fitness points. (4)
  c) Display an alphabetical attendance list (member's name and telephone number) for the spinning class timetabled for 2 January 2018. (4)
  d) Display the number of times member Katie Bradley attended classes in 2017. (3)
  e) Display the name of the trainer 'Ploy Chandra' along with the average fitness points of the classes she has taken. (4)
  f) Display the total number of members each trainer has taught (by trainerName) since the database started recording data on fitness classes. (3)
  g) Display the ID and name of every member who has attended the most expensive class offered by the fitness centre. This requires two steps. (6)
  h) The community centre would like to display the ID and telephone number of members who have 0 fitness points. This requires two steps. (6)

## Chapter 14

Database implementation

At National 5 level, students are expected to create a database with two tables. These tables include a variety of attribute types (text, number, date, time, Boolean) with validation (presence check, restricted choice, field length, range).

In the Higher course there is no requirement to create databases. The entire focus of database implementation is **Structured Query Language (SQL)**.

You will be expected to write the following SQL statements in both the assignment and the exam paper:
- **UPDATE statements** which edit data in two or more fields from one or more tables
- **DELETE statements**
- **INSERT statements**
- **SELECT statements** which make use of multiple tables.

The above statements will make use of wildcards, alias, computed values and aggregate functions.

From design to SQL

Once you have learned to design a query accurately, converting the design to SQL is relatively easy.

Here are a few rules to follow:
1 SELECT
   a) The output from an SQL statement will simply display whatever is listed within SELECT. If we wish to make the output more readable, by including our own headings, an alias is used.
   Design – Member's Name = memberName
   becomes
   SQL – `SELECT memberName AS [Member's Name]`
   b) Where two fields have the same name, dot notation must be used to identify the fields by their table.
   SQL – `Trainer.telNo, Member.telNo`
2 FROM
   The tables listed should include all tables required by any other part of the SQL statement.
3 WHERE
   a) If a query is searching for specific information, this is included as a condition.
   SQL – `WHERE postcode = 'RA6 7DS'`

b) Where a query searches for partial information, wildcards should be used.

SQL – `WHERE memberName LIKE 'Greg%'` (finds any name starting with Greg)

SQL – `WHERE memberName LIKE '%Reid'` (finds any name ending with Reid)

SQL – `WHERE memberName LIKE '_ _ _ _'` (finds any name with exactly four characters)

c) If a query includes fields from more than one table, then a join must be used. This allows the database engine which runs the SQL to identify the link between the data in the tables.

For example, if a query was created to output the names of the members who attended a class on a certain date, the memberName and classDate fields would be required . This would require two joins to link the three tables: Class, Attendance and Member.

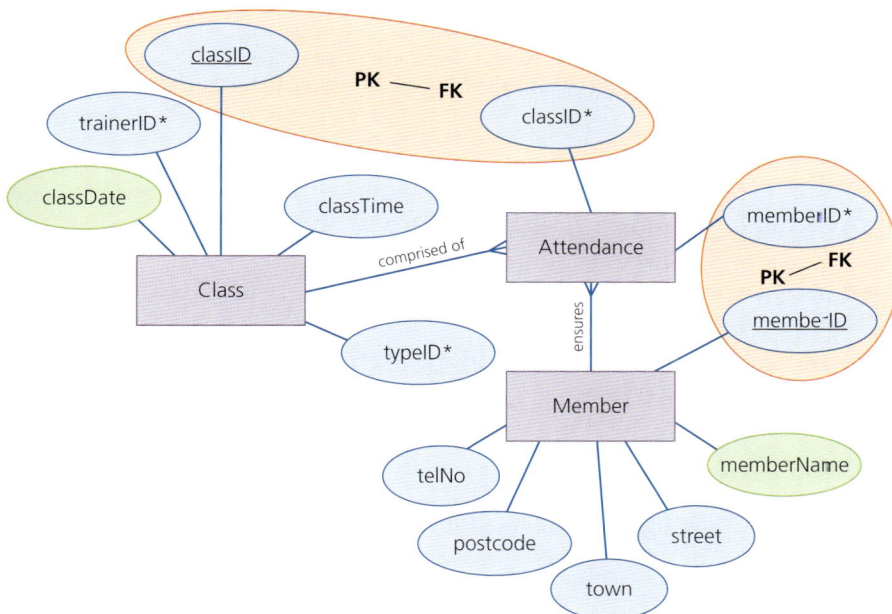

Figure 14.1 Entity relationship diagram showing required joins

SQL – `WHERE Class.classID = Attendance.ClassID AND Attendance.memberID = Member.memberID`

4 GROUP BY

a) When information is grouped by one field, you should avoid selecting other fields to be displayed. For example, you could not group output by surname and also try to display first name at the same time. One instruction tries to create sets of people while the other tries to display individuals. This creates an error.

b) Grouping can be used with aggregate functions. When this is implemented, the function performs a calculation on each grouped set.

Worked examples 🚩

Examples using sample data from the fitness class database

The structure of the community centre fitness class database is shown in Table 14.1 for reference.

Table 14.1 The structure of the community centre fitness class database

Trainer	Class	ClassType	Attendance	Member
trainerID	classID	typeID	memberID*	memberID
trainerName	typeID*	title	classID*	memberName
street	trainerID*	levels		street
town	classDate	description		town
postcode	classTime	durationMin		postcode
hourlyRate		fitnessPoints		telNo
telNo		cost		

The examples below match some of the functional requirements identified in the analysis stage.

Example 1: Update a member's details

Derek Boyle has moved to 34 London Avenue, Whitecliffs, WH546JK. Write an SQL query to change his address.

```
UPDATE Member
SET street = '34 London Avenue', town = 'Whitecliffs', postcode =
'WH546JK'
WHERE memberName = 'Derek Boyle';
```

In Higher, UPDATE queries will involve changing selected values in more than one field. Each change is separated by a comma.

Example 2: Create a list of classes for a single day

Create a list of classes for 14 January 2019, displaying the trainer's name along with the title, time, duration, level and description for each class.

```
SELECT trainerName, title, classTime, durationMin, levels, description
FROM Trainer, Class, ClassType
WHERE classDate = '14/01/2019'
AND Trainer.trainerID = Class.trainerID
AND Class.typeID = ClassType.typeID;
```

The SQL SELECTs the fields to be displayed along with the tables associated with the SELECT and WHERE statements. It searches for a classDate in the Class table. Every aspect of this question is National 5 level except for the double join as three tables are used in the query.

⇨

⇨

Table 14.2 Example 2 query output

trainerName	title	classTime	durationMin	levels	description
Kalem Logan	Spinning	12:30:00	30	Beginner	An introduction to spinning. How best to use the bikes for maximum effectiveness.
Kalem Logan	Zumba	14:00:00	30	Beginner	This is a Zumba class for beginners. The class will include two breaks to catch your breath.
Karen Gilly	CrossFit	14:00:00	45	Intermediate	A mid-intensity class that uses a combination of aerobic exercise, weightlifting and gymnastics to burn calories.

Example 3: Create a list of classes taken by a single trainer for a month along with the money earned for each class

Create a list of classes taken by Davey Jones during May 2019. The class ID and the total money collected for each class should be displayed.

```
SELECT Attendance.classID, SUM(cost) AS [Total Money Collected]
FROM Trainer, Class, ClassType, Attendance
WHERE classDate LIKE '_ _/05/2019'
AND trainerName = 'Davey Jones'
AND Trainer.trainerID = Class.trainerID
AND Class.typeID = ClassType.typeID
AND Class.classID = Attendance.classID
GROUP BY Attendance.classID;
```

The SQL SELECTs the classID from the Attendance table. It GROUPs these so that only one example of each class is shown. For each of these classes a SUM of the cost is calculated.

The WHERE criteria searches for every day in May 2019 (LIKE '_ _/05/2019') using wildcards and the trainer's name. This query uses four tables, meaning that three joins are required in the WHERE criteria to link Trainer, Class, ClassType, Attendance.

Table 14.3 Example 3 query output

classID	Total money collected
4	£35.00
9	£20.00
11	£63.00
14	£10.00

When this query searches for each classID in Attendance, it uses the joins to backtrack to the cost of these classes in ClassType and then SUMs the costs according to how often each classID occurred.

Example 4: Display a sorted list of the members' total fitness points

A prize is to be awarded to the member who has collected the most fitness points (awarded for each class that members attend). Display a sorted list (most points to least points) of each members' total fitness points.

⇨

```
SELECT Member.memberID, memberName, SUM(fitnessPoints) AS [Total
Fitness Points]
FROM Member, Attendance, Class, ClassType
WHERE Class.typeID = ClassType.typeID
AND Class.classID = Attendance.classID
AND Attendance.memberID = Member.memberID
GROUP BY Member.memberID, memberName
ORDER BY SUM(fitnessPoints) DESC;
```

Three joins are required to connect the four tables. The grouping in this example uses both the memberID and the memberName. This is required because:

- using memberID on its own would not display the member's name
- using memberName on its own is not appropriate as two members with the same name would be grouped together.

Note that when grouping is used with a sort, GROUP BY must come before ORDER BY or the database engine will return an error when the SQL is run.

Table 14.4 Example 4 query output

memberID	memberName	Total fitness points
12	Ikra Berg	75
1	Derek Boyle	70
6	Imran Worthington	69
3	Cary Bryant	64
13	Katherine Dejesus	60
2	Josie Tarrent	48
4	Jeremy Softie	47
7	Jennie Mccall	45
5	Nayla Delagado	44
10	Elizabeth Pugh	42
8	Aariz Wilcox	31
9	Bree Montes	27
14	Frank Turner	25
15	Cindy Webb	22
11	Dainton Waters	5

Example 5: Display a list of the most expensive classes

Write an SQL statement to find the most expensive class and then display the titles and levels of every class that costs the same as the most expensive class.

The answer requires two SQL statements.

First find the maximum cost:

```
SELECT MAX(cost) AS mostExpensive
FROM ClassType;
```

Table 14.5 Example 5 query output 1

Query1
mostExpensive
10.00

Then use this value in the second SQL statements:

```
SELECT title, levels
FROM ClassType, Query1
WHERE cost = mostExpensive;
```

Table 14.6 Example 5 query output 2

title	levels
Spinning	Advanced
HIIT	Advanced

What you should know 👍

In your revision of this chapter, ensure that you are able to:

★ write an SQL statement using examples for reference
★ explain the purpose of an alias
★ understand the effect of wildcards on searches
★ understand the need to link tables using joins
★ explain the purpose of aggregate functions
★ explain the effect of grouping.

Questions ❓

For each of the following questions, write an SQL statement to create the required output from the fitness class database. You may wish to design the queries first.

1 Change the street and telephone number of trainer 'Joyce Bryant' to '6 Woodburn Terrace' and '07964388472'. (3)
2 Display the title and level of all the classes that contain the phrase 'no breaks' in the fitness class description. (3)
3 Calculate how much trainer 'Derek Hawk' should be paid for taking the only 10 a.m. class on 29 December 2018. (6)
4 Calculate the average number of fitness points earned by member 'Zubair Samuels' over all the classes he attended in 2018. (8)
5 Display the cheapest and dearest classes attended by member 'Jean Smith'. (7)
6 Display a list of each classID, with its title, showing the total number of members that attended each fitness class. Sort the results from highest to lowest attendance. (6)

⇨

7 Use two SQL statements to calculate and display the total wages earned by trainer 'Robert Hightower' in March 2019. (9)

In an exam you may alsc be asked to read SQL statements and explain their purpose. For each of the following questions, describe the output produced when the SQL is run.

8 (2)

```
SELECT title, levels
FROM Trainer, Class, ClassType
WHERE trainerName = 'Bo Jackson'
AND Trainer.trainerID = Class.trainerID
AND Class.typeID = ClassType.typeID;
```

9 (2)

```
SELECT title, classDate
FROM Member, Attendance, Class, ClassType
WHERE memberName LIKE 'Jill%'
AND Member.memberID = Attendance.memberID
AND Attendance.classID = Class.classID
AND Class.typeID = ClassType.typeID;
```

10 (2)

```
SELECT Member.memberID, memberName, SUM(durationMin)
FROM Member, Attendance, Class, ClassType
WHERE Class.typeID = ClassType.typeID
AND Class.classID = Attendance.classID
AND Attendance.memberID = Member.memberID
GROUP BY Member.memberID, memberName;
```

## Chapter 15

Database testing

When testing SQL statements, it is important to ensure that they run without error (in other words the syntax is correct) and produce the expected output. In an exam you may be asked one of the following types of questions.

Example 1 🚩

Describe how you would you test the following SQL statement

Describe how the following SQL statement could be tested to ensure the output it produces is correct. (3)

```
SELECT customerName, SUM(itemCost)
FROM Customer, Order, OrderLine
WHERE orderNo = 997664
AND Customer.customerID = Order.customerID
AND Order.orderNo = OrderLine.orderNo;
```

When answering a question like this, focus on the search and display elements of the SQL.

Solution

To test this SQL statement I would look for all the items relating to order number 997664 and manually add up their costs. I would also look for the name of the customer who placed the order. Finally, I would run the SQL statement to see if the actual output matches the expected output, as predicted by the manual search and calculation.

Example 2 🚩

Explain why the SQL statement below would not give the required output when tested

The SQL statement below is written to display a list of customers, with their ID and names appearing only once, who placed orders in June 2019. (2)

```
SELECT customerID, customerName
FROM Customer, Order
WHERE orderDate LIKE "_ _/06/_ _ _ _"
AND Customer.customerID = Order.customerID;
```

When answering questions like this, focus on finding something in the SQL that will produce output that doesn't match the requirements.

Solution

The SQL statement will find orders from June of any year, not just 2019. The output should have been grouped so that only one example of each customer's ID and name was displayed.

Example 3

Find the error in the SQL statement below

This SQL statement will not run when tested. Assuming that all field names are correct, state the errors in the SQL code. (3)

```
SELECT itemName, itemQuantity, itemCost
FROM Order, OrderLine
WHERE orderNo = "997664"
AND orderNo = orderNo
```

Solution

orderNo = "997664" does not require inverted commas as this is a number. The table names are missing from the join. The whole statement has not been finished with a semi-colon.

What you should know

In your revision of this chapter, ensure that you are able to:

★ explain the purpose of testing SQL statements
★ explain how a specific SQL statement would be tested to ensure accurate output
★ find output errors in working SQL statements
★ find syntax errors in SQL statements.

Questions

Each of the questions below refers to the fitness class database. For each question, describe how you would test the SQL statement.

1 (2)

```
UPDATE ClassType
SET durationMin = 60, cost = 9.00
WHERE title = 'Spinning' AND levels = 'Intermediate';
```

2 (2)

```
SELECT Class.trainerID, COUNT(*)
FROM Class
GROUP BY Class.trainerID;
```

3 (3)

```
SELECT memberName
FROM Class, Attendance, Member
WHERE  Class.classID = 5
AND Class.classID = Attendance.classID
AND Attendance.memberID = Member.memberID
ORDER BY memberName;
```

⇨

⇨

For each of the following questions explain why the required output/change may not be achieved.

4 An SQL statement is written to add 10% to the cost of every spinning class. (2)

```
UPDATE ClassType
SET cost = cost*0.1
WHERE title LIKE "S%";
```

5 An SQL statement is written to display the average price of fitness classes. (2)

```
SELECT typeID, AVG(durationMin)
FROM ClassType
GROUP BY typeID;
```

6 An SQL statement is written to display the amount of money collected from members for a single fitness class that took place on 12 March 2019 at 10 a.m. (2)

```
SELECT SUM(cost) AS [Class Takings]
FROM Class, ClassType
WHERE classDate = "12/03/2019" AND classTime = "10:00"
AND Class.typeID = ClassType.typeID;
```

For each of the following questions identify the syntax errors that would prevent the SQL statement from running without errors/user input.

7 (2)

```
SELECT title, levels, description
FROM ClassType, Class, Member
WHERE memberID = 23
AND Class.typeID = ClassType.typeID
AND Class.classID = Attendance.classID
AND Attendance.memberID = Member.memberID;
```

8 (2)

```
SELECT trainerID, trainerName, AVG(fitnessPoints)
FROM Trainer, Class, ClassType
WHERE Class.typeID = ClassType.typeID
AND Trainer.trainerID = Class.classID
GROUP BY trainerID;
```

9 (3)

```
SELECT Attendance.classID, SUM(cost)
FROM ClassType, Class, Attendance, Member
AND Class.typeID = ClassType.typeID
AND Class.classID = Attendance.classID
AND Attendance.memberID = Member.memberID;
ORDER BY SUM(cost)
GROUP BY Attendance.classID;
```

## Chapter 16

Database evaluation

Fitness for purpose

A database is fit for purpose if it meets the functional requirements identified at the analysis stage. Remember the functional requirements are a list of the data that should be stored and the queries that should be performed on this data.

Worked example 🚩

Community centre fitness classes

The database was required to store a list of given data on trainers, fitness classes and members. The database includes tables and fields that store all the required data.

The database was required to perform the following functions:

- insert/delete/update a member's details
- insert/delete/update a trainer's details
- insert/delete/update a class
- insert/delete/update a class register
- create a list of classes (trainer's name, title, time, duration, level, description) for a single day
- create a list of classes taken by a single trainer for a month along with the money earned for each class
- generate the total pay due to a trainer for one month's classes
- generate the total money paid by members for classes at the end of each day
- display a sorted list of the members' total fitness points
- display a list of the most expensive classes.

Each of the above was implemented successfully.

The fitness class database meets the set of requirements so can be said to be fit for purpose.

Accuracy of output

The accuracy of output from a database will relate to:

- the accuracy of the data itself (whether it is kept up to date)
- the correctness of any SQL queries implemented (a mistake in an SQL calculation, for example, could result in inaccurate output)
- the effect of any updates.

Worked example 🚩

Community centre fitness classes

Testing showed that updating the cost for a class type meant that all previous similar classes now cost the newly updated amount. The previous classes had a different cost on the day the class took place. The design and implementation of the cost attribute has created inaccurate output.

If the cost field was moved from the classType table and included in the Class table instead, then each new Class record would have its own cost. This would allow the cost of a particular type of class to change over time.

What you should know 👍

In your revision of this chapter, ensure that you are able to:

★ explain what makes a database fit for purpose
★ understand that decisions made around how data is organised and maintained may affect the accuracy of output.

Questions ❓

1 If the fitness class database had also included a functional requirement to record whether or not a member had paid for a fitness class, it would not have been fit for purpose when it was evaluated.

Describe how you could edit the database tables to ensure that the member payment information was correctly stored by the database. (3)

2 A database was fit for purpose when it was created in 2013 but is now not fit for purpose. State what could have caused this. (1)

Area 4 Web Design and Development

## Chapter 17

Web analysis

When creating a website for a client, interviews are conducted, information is gathered and examples of documents, photographs, etc. are collated.

The purpose of this is to define the end-user and functional requirements of the website.

End-user requirements are what the client and the eventual users of the website would like to see in the finished site.

Functional requirements are the functions and facilities that the website code must provide in order to meet the client/users' requirements.

What you should know 👍

In your revision of this chapter, ensure that you are able to:
★ explain the difference between end-user and functional requirements
★ identify end-user and functional requirements of a web-based problem.

Questions ?

1 A bathroom supplier hires a web development company to create a new website. The web developers discuss the new site with the company's employees. Statements made by the employees are listed below:
   ○ 'In our shop, customers are looking for one of four things: toilets, baths, showers and sinks. It is important that the website shows many pictures of all of these products along with the price of each.'
   ○ 'Toilets can either be attached to a wall or sit on the floor. Some modern toilets have no rims.'
   ○ 'Customers might like to see a video showing how the different settings on a whirlpool bath can be used to create bubbles or water jets.'
   ○ 'Some showers are electric, some are just complete units that run from a water tank. We sell a variety of enclosures to stand in when having a shower.'
   ○ 'Sinks can be attached to a wall or stand on a pillar called a pedestal.'
   Identify two end-user and two functional requirements from the employees' statements. (2)

## Chapter 18

Web design

A complete design for a website may include the following:
- a website structure diagram showing the pages in the website and their logical connections
- wireframe designs showing how the content of each page is laid out
- form designs showing layout and user inputs expected
- low-fidelity prototypes showing mock-ups of each page used in user testing.

Website structure

At Higher you will be expected to implement a multi-level website where each main page may link to one or more sub-pages on that topic. A **structure diagram** lists the main pages and sub-pages that will be included in the website.

A website structure diagram for a bathroom supplies company website is shown below.

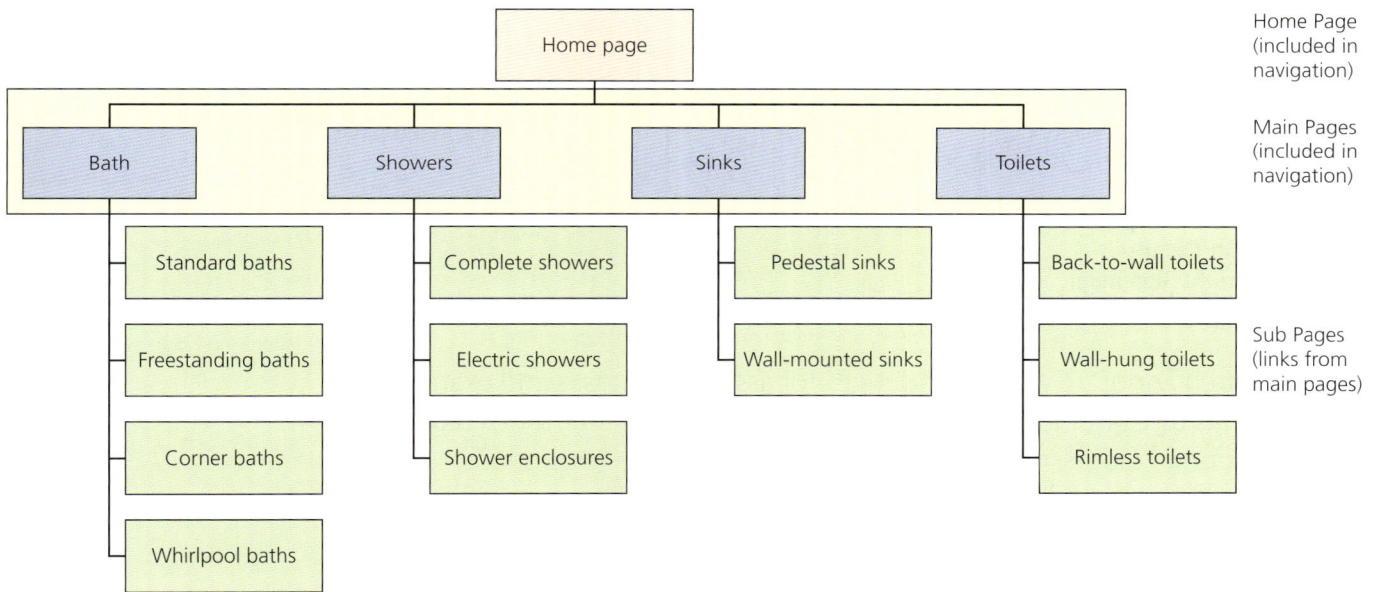

Figure 18.1 Website structure diagram

The coloured area highlights the main pages (topics) in the website. These will be included within the navigation bar of the website when it is implemented.

Links will be created from the main pages to each of the sub-pages.

Wireframe designs

Wireframe designs may be very basic, showing simple labelled boxes, or quite detailed, including precise widths and heights of content as well as the spaces between different content.

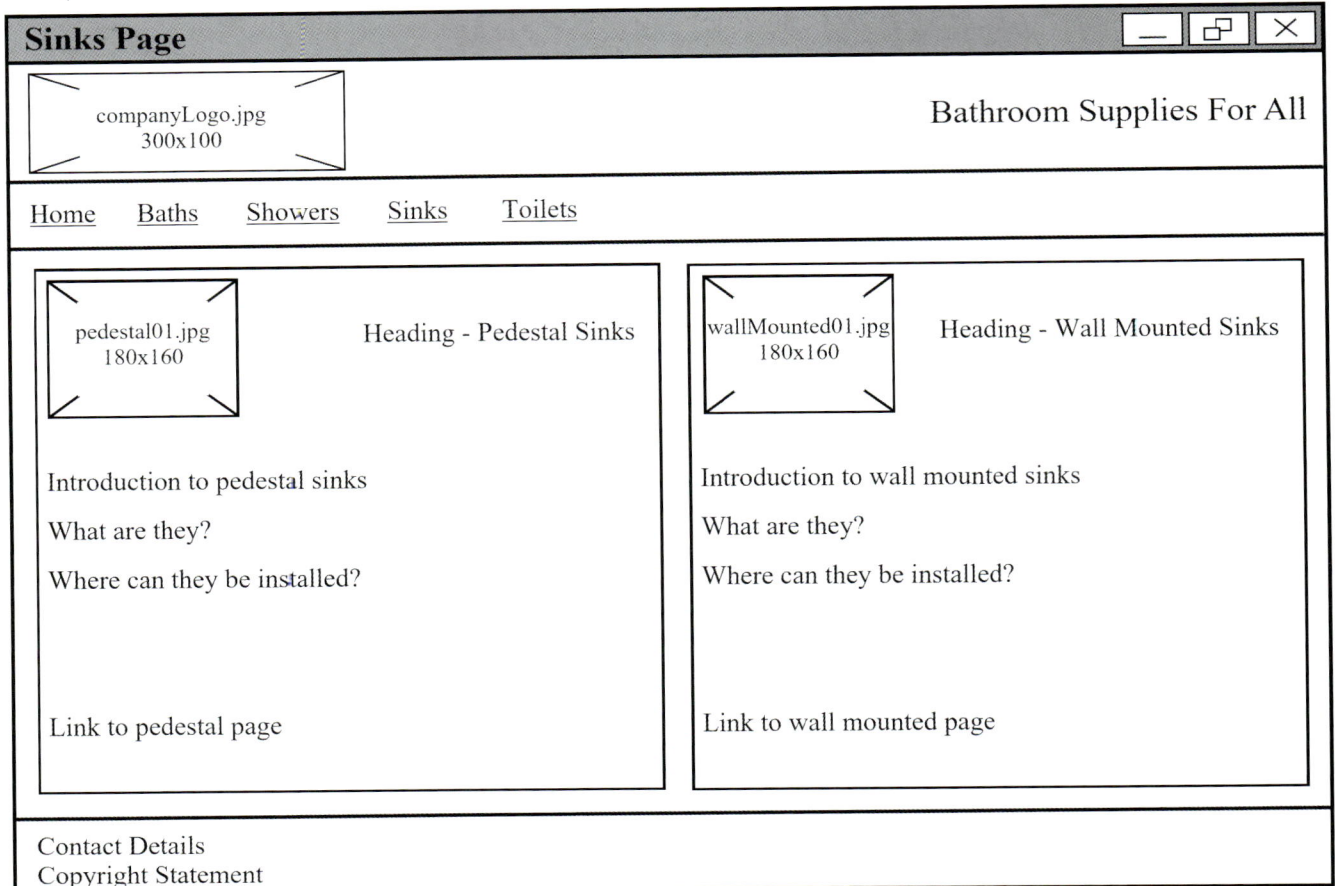

Figure 18.2 A wireframe design

SQA often annotate wireframe designs for assignment tasks and exam questions. The additional information may include text size/font/colour, background colours, margins, paddings and interactive instructions.

Form design

The design of a **form** should clearly show:

- the inputs required along with their type (text, numeric, text area, drop-down selection menu or radio buttons)
- instructions that may be given to the user (these may serve a secondary purpose of describing the input on the design)
- any validation to be implemented (length check of characters, numeric range or presence check for unwanted empty inputs)
- any pre-assigned values.

SQA have provided examples of how they will present form design in an exam question or assignment task. An example of this is shown in Figure 18.3.

```
World Championships feedback form

  ┌──────────────────────────────────────────────────────────────┐
  │ Name - text input box - max size 20 characters - default to    │
  │ 'anonymous' - required                                         │
  └──────────────────────────────────────────────────────────────┘

  ┌──────────────────────────────────────────────────────┬─────┐
  │ Drop down menu to pick event attended.  Default to     │  ▼  │
  │ track&field.                                           │     │
  │ (track & field, cycling, rowing, hockey, football,     │     │
  │ archery)                                               │     │
  └──────────────────────────────────────────────────────┴─────┘

  ┌──────────────────────────────────────────────────────────────┐
  │ Rate venue's facilities (1 poor, 10 excellent)- numeric input  │
  │ - range from 1 to 10 -  required                              │
  └──────────────────────────────────────────────────────────────┘

  ┌──────────────────────────────────────────────────────────────┐
  │ Describe any improvements you would like to see in the venue.  │
  │ text area box - max 180 characters - not required             │
  │                                                                │
  │                                                                │
  └──────────────────────────────────────────────────────────────┘

  ┌──────────────────────────────────────────────────────────────┐
  │ Did you drive to the event - default 'No'                      │
  │   ◯ Yes          ⦿ No                                         │
  └──────────────────────────────────────────────────────────────┘

  ┌──────────────────────────────────────────────────────────────┐
  │ How much did your parking cost? - numeric input - min = 0 -    │
  │ default to 0 - required                                        │
  └──────────────────────────────────────────────────────────────┘

  ( Submit )
```

Figure 18.3 Form design

Low-fidelity prototypes

A **prototype** is a mock-up of a web page either drawn on paper by hand or created using software and printed. The '**low-fidelity**' refers to the prototype containing only basic information. Prototypes can be shown to clients to give them an initial idea of what pages may look like when they are implemented.

What you should know 👍

In your revision of this chapter, ensure that you are able to:
★ explain the purpose of each type of design
★ create designs from end-user and functional requirements identified in analysis
★ explain the roles of designs when discussing a proposed website with a client.

Questions ?

1 State why wireframe designs do not include all of the content for each page. (1)
2 Describe the relationship between the website structure navigation and implementing a navigation bar. (2)
3 a) State two restricted-choice input types used on form designs. (2)
  b) Which of these input types restricts the user to only one input. (1)
4 Explain how a text area input could be designated 'required' but not actually require the user to input any text. (1)
5 State what happens next if a client says they do not like the look of a low-fidelity prototype design. (2)

## Chapter 19

Web implementation

At Higher level, you are required to code a website using three different technologies:

- **Hypertext Markup Language (HTML)**: used to define the structure and content of each web page.
- **Cascading Style Sheets (CSS)**: used to describe how HTML elements will be displayed.
- **JavaScript (JS)**: used to add interactivity to web pages.

HTML 5 page structure

HTML 5 provides elements that may be used to structure the content of a page.

The **<header>** element is used at the top of the page and usually contains contents that will appear on every web page in the website. This is often called a **banner**.

The **<nav>** element contains the navigation/hyperlinks to the main pages that will appear on every web page. Links could be a simple vertical list or a horizontal navigation bar.

The **<main>** element contains the content of the page. This will be different for every page. Content within the <main> element may be split up using **<section>** elements. A <section> is used to define an area of related content, for example a photograph with a description of the photo.

The **<footer>** element usually contains contact information and legal information. This content also appears on every page.

An element that has other elements inside it is called a **container**. The term 'container' is not part of Higher but it is part of the language of web coding.

Web coders rarely write code from scratch, preferring to start with template files as shown in Figure 19.1.

```
<!DOCTYPE html>
<html>

<head>
    <title>     </title>
    <link rel="stylesheet" type="text/css" href="../CSS/   .css">
</head>

<body>

    <!-- Page Header/Banner -->
    <header>

    </header>

    <!-- Navigation Bar -->
    <nav>

    </nav>

    <!-- The main content of the page -->
    <main>

    </main>

    <!-- Page Footer -->
    <footer>

    </footer>

</body>

</html>
```

Figure 19.1 Basic web structure (HTML 5)

Cascading Style Sheets

Efficient coding using grouping and descendant selectors

Higher not only introduces new Cascading Style Sheets (CSS) properties but requires that code is written efficiently.

A **grouping selector** allows the coder to combine CSS declarations, reducing the amount of code required. For example:

Table 19.1 Using a grouping selector

Before (separate code)	After (grouping)
nav {margin-top:5px}	nav, main, footer, p {margin-top:5px}
main {margin-top:5px}	
footer {margin-top:5px}	
p {margin-top:5px}	

Grouped selectors are separated by commas.

Descendant selectors are used to reduce the need for IDs and classes by further defining the position of the element to be styled. For example:

Table 19.2 Using descendant selectors

Coding using descendant selectors	Alternative version using classes
section p {font-size:10px;color:black}	.sectionParagraphs {font-size:10px;colcr:black}
footer p {font-size:10px;color:darkBlue}	.footerParagraphs {font-size:10px;color:darkBlue}
p {font-size:12px;color:black}	p {font-size:12px;color:black}

The above styles would be applied to:
- <p> elements contained within a <section> element
- <p> elements contained within a <footer> element
- any other <p> elements.

If classes were used instead to assign these styles, then extra code would be required in the HTML file to assign the classes to every appropriate element throughout the website.

Controlling appearance (display)

The CSS 'display' property has three values: **block**, **inline** and **none**. Each of these changes how an element appears on a page.

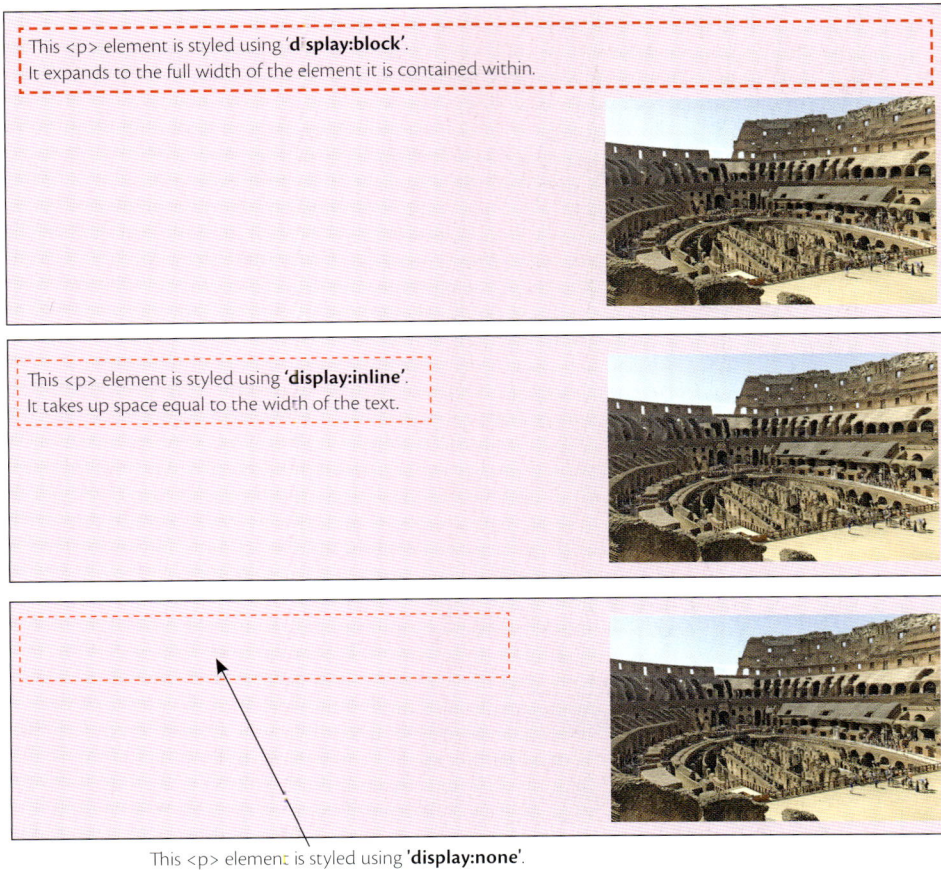

> This <p> element is styled using '**display:block**'.
> It expands to the full width of the element it is contained within.

> This <p> element is styled using '**display:inline**'.
> It takes up space equal to the width of the text.

This <p> element is styled using '**display:none**'.

Figure 19.2 Display examples

Where no styles are applied, different elements will default to either block (<div> <h1>-<h6> <p> <form> <header> <footer> <section>) or inline (<a> <img>).

When an element is styled using display:block, it becomes impossible to position another element, within the same container, beside it.

The display property is often used with JavaScript to hide (none) or show (block/inline) page content.

Controlling the space between elements (margins and padding)

The distance between elements on a page can be controlled using margins and padding.

Margins are used to push an element away from another element or in from the edge of a container.

The Colosseum is an amphitheatre, situated just east of the Roman Forum, in the centre of Rome, Italy. Built of travertine with a brick face, it is the largest amphitheatre ever built. Construction was started by emperor Vespasian in AD 72 and was completed in AD 80 by his successor, Titus.

margin:5px

\<section\> container

margin:10px   margin:20px

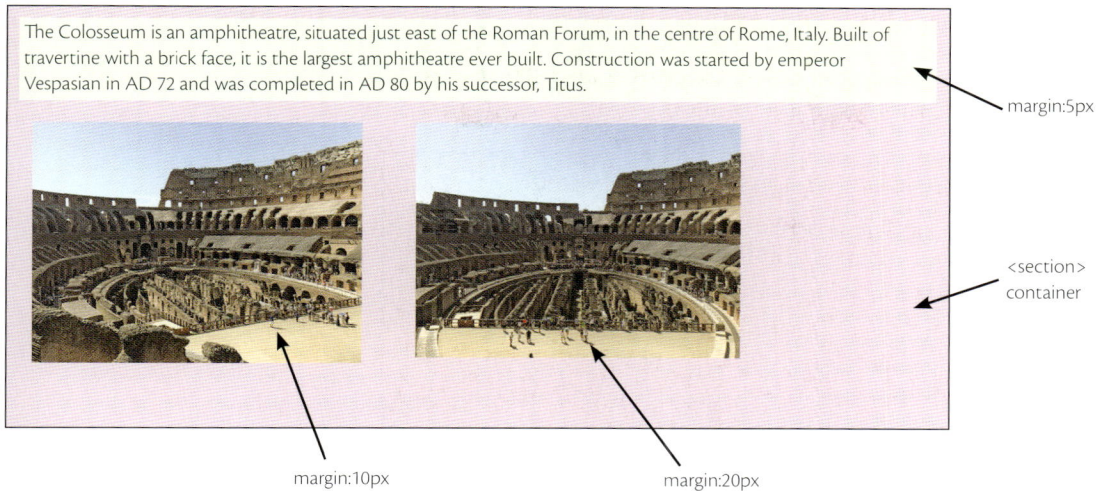

Figure 19.3 Margin examples

Note that margins push away from other elements and not from other margins. Margins overlap rather than combine. The space between the text and the left-hand photo in Figure 19.3 is 10 pixels (not 5 + 10 as you might expect).

Padding pushes content in from the edge of an element. This is often used with \<p\> elements to create some space around the text or with containers to move every object in from the edge of the container element.

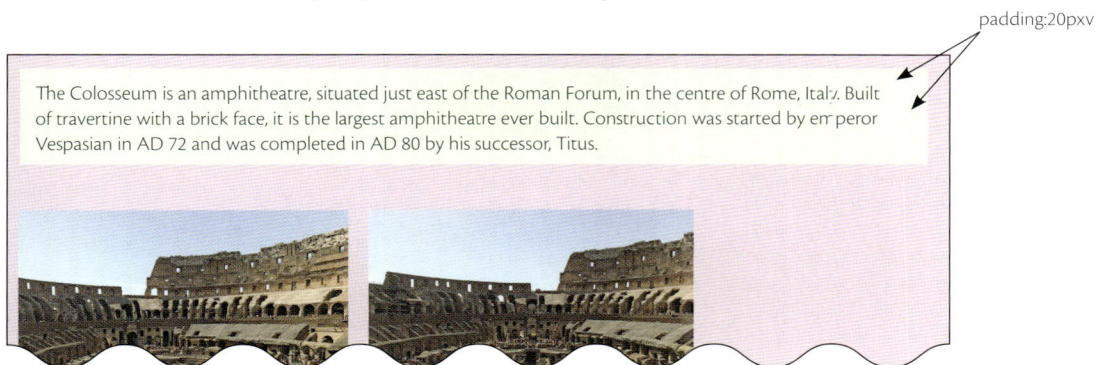

padding:20pxv

The Colosseum is an amphitheatre, situated just east of the Roman Forum, in the centre of Rome, Italy. Built of travertine with a brick face, it is the largest amphitheatre ever built. Construction was started by emperor Vespasian in AD 72 and was completed in AD 80 by his successor, Titus.

Figure 19.4 Padding examples

Margins and padding may be declared individually:

```
margin-left:10px; margin-bottom:10px;
margin-top:10px; margin-right:10px
```

or grouped to apply the margin to every side of the element:

```
margin:10px
```

Sizing elements (width, height)

The width and height of many elements will expand and contract when the size of a browser window is changed. To permanently fix the size of an element it can be styled using the CSS width and height properties.

```
width:600px; height:200px
```

Floating elements (float, clear)

Without styling, a browser will usually display elements vertically down a page.

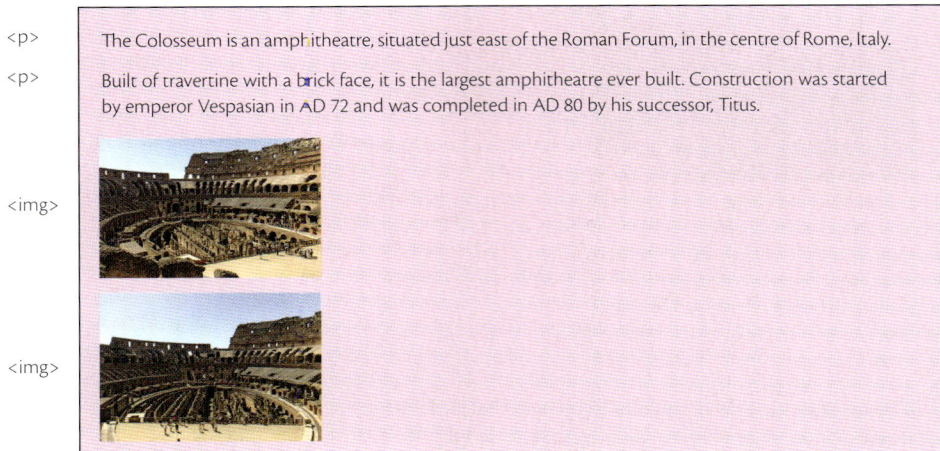

Figure 19.5 No floating

To display two elements beside each other, one of the elements is styled using the '**float**' property. When an element is floated, other elements wrap around the floated element.

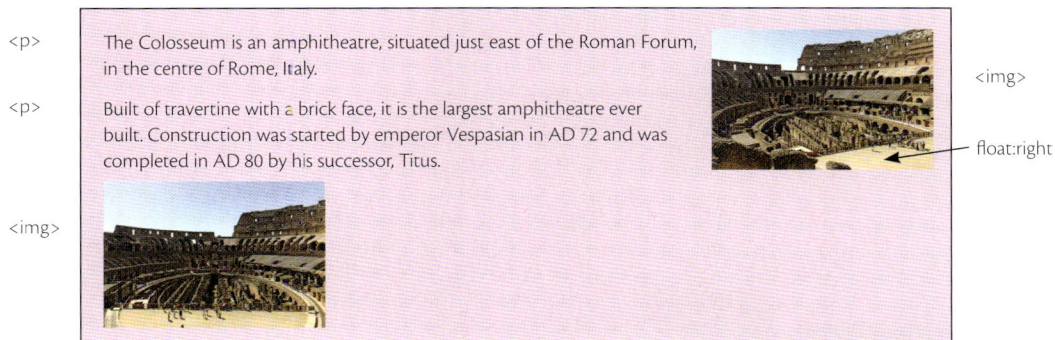

Figure 19.6 With floating

Note how the floated image affects both paragraphs, with both wrapping around the image.

The effect of a float style can be cancelled. If, for example, we wished the second paragraph to start after the floated image, we can cancel the effect of float by adding the '**clear:both**' style to the second paragraph. This has the effect of forcing the paragraph to start after the image.

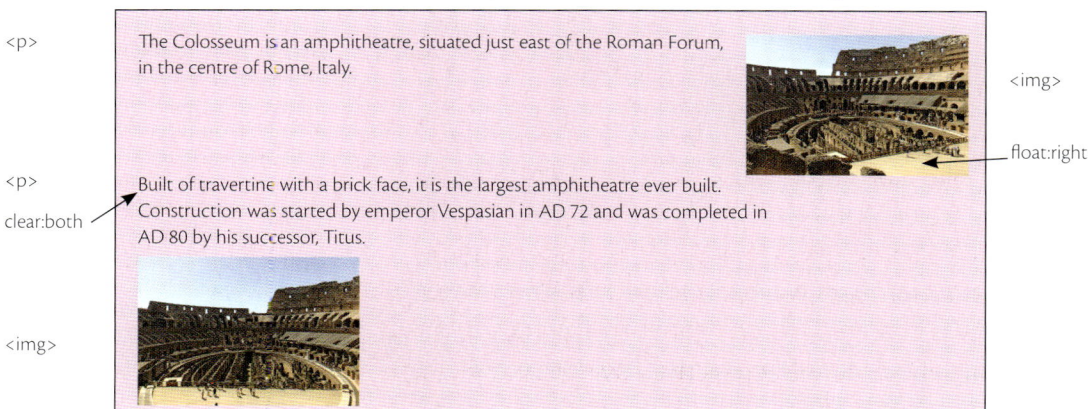

Figure 19.7 Float with clear

Styling a navigation bar (list-style-type:none, hover)

A **navigation bar** is effectively a row of clickable boxes, each of which is a hyperlink to another page. This can be created by styling an unordered list to appear as a navigation bar.

First the hyperlinks are added as an unordered list to the <nav> element of the HTML file.

```
<nav>
    <ul>
        <li><a href="home.html">Home</a></li>
        <li><a href="colosseum.html">Colosseum</a></li>
        <li><a href="romanForum.html">Roman Forum</a></li>
        <li><a href="treviFountain.html">Trevi Fountain</a></li>
        <li><a href="pantheon.html">Pantheon</a></li>
    </ul>
</nav>
```

Figure 19.8 Navigation list

When viewed in a browser, with no styles, the list looks like this.

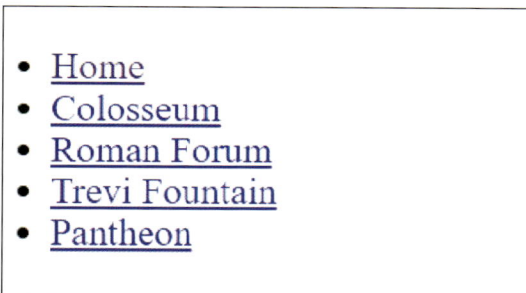

- Home
- Colosseum
- Roman Forum
- Trevi Fountain
- Pantheon

Figure 19.9 Navigation list in browser

To change the appearance and behaviour of the list to that of a navigation bar, the following code is added. Note the use of descendant selectors to ensure the styles are only applied to a list within the navigation bar.

```
nav {height:35px;background-color:lightblue;font-size:12pt}
nav ul {list-style-type:none}
nav ul li {float:left;width:120px;text-align:center}
nav ul li a {display:block;padding:8px}
nav ul li a:hover {background-color:black;color:white}
```

Figure 19.10 CSS for navigation bar

This code can be broken down as follows:
- "background-color:lightblue" and "font-size:12pt" set the colour and text size for the navigation element
- "list-style-type:none" is used to hide the bullets in the <ul> element
- "height:35px" and "width:120px" are used to set the <li> elements as a box 120 × 35
- "float:left" is used to stack all the boxes across the navigation bar from left to right
- "text-align:center" and "padding:8px" are used to position the text in the middle of each box

- "display:block" ensures that the whole box becomes a clickable link and not just the text
- a:hover {background-color:black;color:white} is used to change the colour of a box when the mouse pointer hovers over a link.

When this code is implemented, the navigation bar looks like this:

| Home | Colosseum | Roman Forum | Trevi Fountain | Pantheon |

Figure 19.11 Navigation bar in browser

Forms

The Higher course introduces the concept of HTML 5 forms. Usually a form would allow the user to submit information to a server but this is not required at Higher. (Server side form handling is covered in Advanced Higher.)

An example of an HTML 5 form, along with how the form looks in a browser, is shown in Figures 19.12 and 19.13.

```html
<form action="">
    First name:<br>
    <input type="text" name="firstname" size="30" maxlength="15" required>
    <br>

    Last name:<br>
    <input type="text" name="lastname" size="30" maxlength="15" required>
    <br><br>

    Select attraction:
    <select name="attraction" multiple size="3">
        <option value="colos" selected>Colosseum</option>
        <option value="roma">Roman Forum</option>
        <option value="trevi">Trevi Fountain</option>
        <option value="panth">Pantheon</option>
    </select>
    <br><br>

    Number of tickets required (between 1 and 8):
    <input type="number" name="tickets" value="1" min="1" max="8">
    <br><br>

    Choose your ticket type:<br>
    <input type="radio" name="type" value="day" checked> day
    <input type="radio" name="type" value="week"> week
    <input type="radio" name="type" value="year"> year
    <br><br>

    Do you require assistance when you are visiting our attractions?<br>
    If yes, please supply details below.<br>
    <textarea name="assistance" rows="2" cols="50">none</textarea>
    <br><br>

    <input type="submit" value="Submit">
</form>
```

Figure 19.12 Form example code

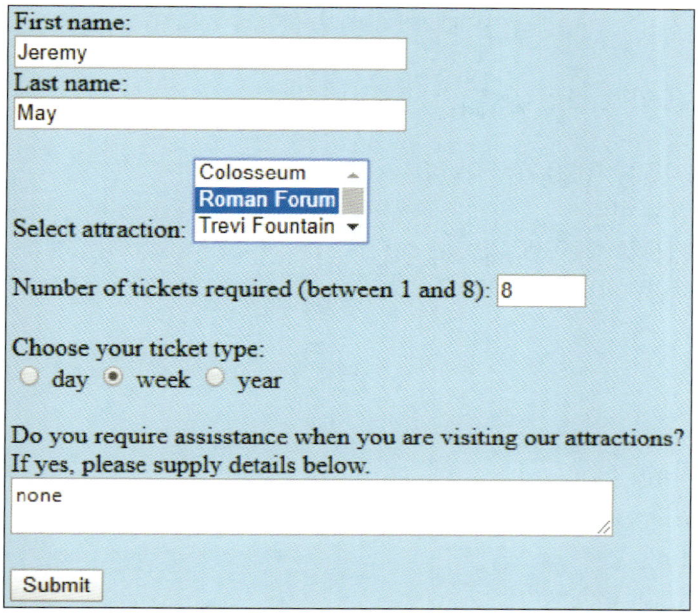

First name:
Jeremy
Last name:
May

Select attraction: Colosseum / Roman Forum / Trevi Fountain

Number of tickets required (between 1 and 8): 8

Choose your ticket type:
○ day ● week ○ year

Do you require assisstance when you are visiting our attractions?
If yes, please supply details below.
none

Submit

Figure 19.13 Form viewed in browser

The form code can be explained as follows:
- The <form> </form> element encloses all of the form code.
- The form can contain text instructions to the user as well as the input types listed below:
  - type="text" – a simple text box
  - select – a drop-down menu where one or more options can be chosen
  - type="number" – input of a number
  - type="radio" – radio buttons where one option can be chosen
  - textarea – a box allowing longer text input.
- Inputs can be validated.
- Inputs can be given default values:
  - select – a pre-chosen default is set using "selected"
  - type="text"/"number" – a default is set using the "value" attribute
  - type="radio" – a pre-selected default is set using "checked"
  - textarea – the element can enclose text that will appear in the box when the page loads.
- The form should have a submit button.
- The inclusion, or not, of <br> elements can be used to control whether content appears side-by-side or below on the next line.

Form validation

HTML 5 provides the functionality to check that form inputs are valid, without the need for JavaScript code.
- **Length check**: The maximum number of characters that can be entered into a text box is set using the "maxlength" property. This is different from "size" which sets the physical size of the box.
- **Range check**: The min and max attributes are added to numeric input to set a range.
- **Presence check**: Input attributes can be set to "required" to ensure the form is not submitted with required input missing.

JavaScript

Events

When JavaScript code is added to a web page, it is often triggered by an event. The three events included in the Higher course are:

- **onmouseover** – when the mouse passes over a page element
- **onmouseout** – when the mouse moves away from an element
- **onclick** – when the user clicks on an element.

Events are placed within HTML elements:

```
<img src="reveal.png" onClick=" ">
```

What can JavaScript do?

JavaScript, in Higher Computing, is limited to changing the style of an element. This can be achieved in three ways:

1 Referring to "this"

```
<img src="dog.jpg" onMouseOver="this.style.width='150px';this.style.
height='150px'" onMouseOut="this.style.width='100px';this.style.
height='100px'">
```

The highlighted text can be broken down to:

- this – the element containing the JavaScript event which is <img src="dog.jpg">
- style – a style change will be applied to "this" element
- width='150px' – the CSS style that will be applied
- multiple JavaScript instructions are separated by a semi-colon ';'.

2 Referring to an element id

```
<img id="dog1" src="dog.jpg"
onMouseOver="document.getElementById('dog1').style.height='150px';
document.getElementById('dog1').style.width='100px';document.
getElementById('dog1').style.height='100px'">
```

The highlighted text can again be broken down:

- id="dog1" – the element is given a unique id to identify it
- document.getElementById([So, ()]) – the JavaScript function document.getElementById('dog1') finds the element with the id 'dog1'.

This method is useful if the JavaScript is to style a different element from the one containing the event.

3 Calling a function

JavaScript code can be written within functions which can be placed anywhere within the HTML file (but usually in the <head> element). The JavaScript is placed within <script> elements.

```
<script>
    function displayDog1() {
    document.getElementById("dog1").style.display="block";
    document.getElementById("dog2").style.display="none";
    }
</script>
```

The function can then be called by the event.

```
<img id="dog1" src="dog.jpg">
<img id="dog2" src="dog.jpg">
<img src="button.jpg" onClick="function displayDog1()">
```

Clicking 'button.jpg' changes the 'display' style of the two images to show dog1 image and hide dog2.

Functions are usually used when:
- an event triggers several lines of code
- the same code is called from multiple events.

Using the above code, JavaScript could be used on a page to:
- make images increase or decrease in size
- change the colour, size or font of text
- hide and show various page elements using display; this could be a single image or a whole section
- change where an image is positioned by floating it to a different place.

What you should know 👍

In your revision of this chapter, ensure that you are able to:
- ★ explain the different purposes of HTML, CSS and JavaScript
- ★ explain the purpose of the HTML 5 elements: header, nav, main, section, footer
- ★ write CSS rules using grouping and descendant selectors
- ★ explain the effect of CSS rules including: display, margins, padding, width, height, float and clear
- ★ write CSS rules to style a navigation bar
- ★ write HTML code to create a form with range, length and presence validation
- ★ explain the effect of the JavaScript events: onmouseover, onmouseout and onclick
- ★ write JavaScript code to change the style of page objects
- ★ write JavaScript functions.

Questions ?

1 Rewrite the CSS selectors, properties and values below to make the code more efficient. (2)

```
header {padding-left:5px; padding-right:5px;
padding-bottom:5px; padding-top:5px}
header {font-size:12px}
nav {padding:5px, font-size:12px}
main {padding:20px}
main {font-size:10px}
footer {padding:5px; font-size:12px}
```

2 The annotated wireframe below shows the <main> element containing three <section> elements from the showers page of the bathroom supplier's website. Each <section> element has been assigned an id.

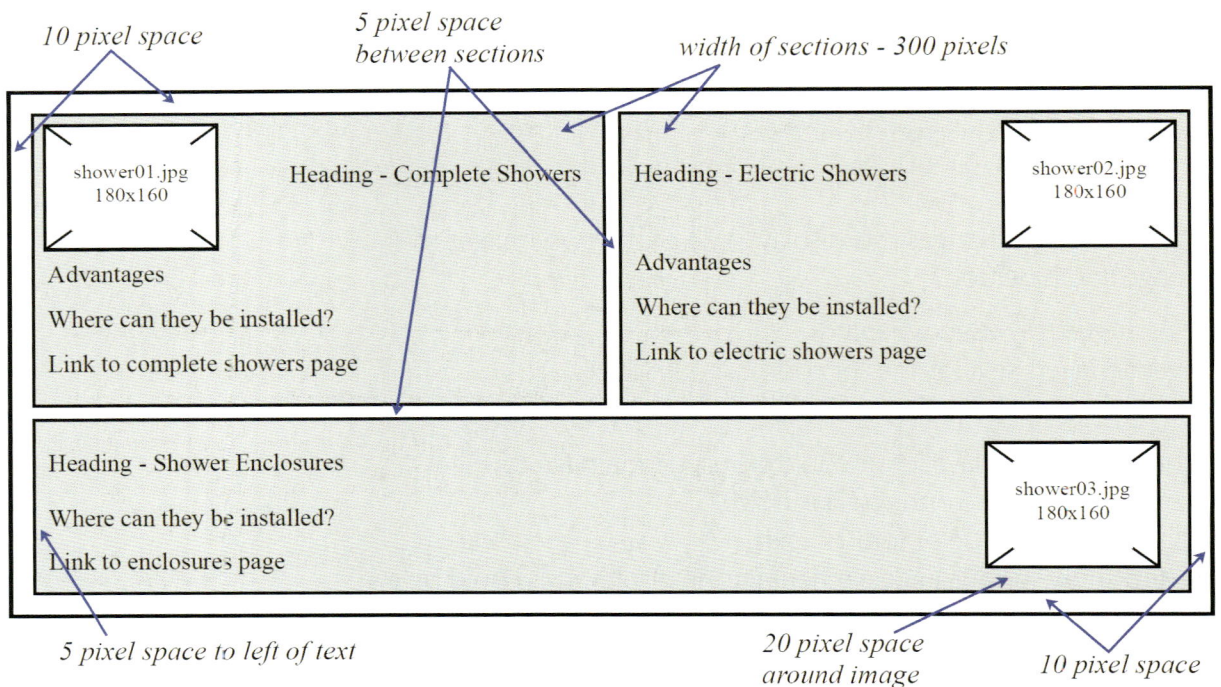

Figure 19.14 Shower page <main>

A CSS file is created to style the elements of this page. It contains the following selectors:

```
main {      }
#complete   {     }
#electric   {     }
#enclosures   {     }
```

   a) Copy and complete the above code to style the 10-pixel space around the three <section> elements. (2)
   b) Copy and complete the above code to style the 5-pixel spaces between the three <section>s. (2)
   c) Explain how the wireframe shows that 'shower03.jpg' must be styled with margins. (1)
3 Look at the example wireframe 'Sinks page' given as Figure 18.2 in the previous chapter. Describe where the CSS float property would have to be used to position content if this page were implemented. (4)
4 Using the shower page wireframe from question 1, describe where "clear:both" should be styled. (2)

⇨

⇒

5 The code below is written to style a navigation bar.

```
/* Navigation List Properties */
nav {height:50px;background-color:lightblue;font-size:10pt}
nav ul {list-style-type:none}
nav ul li {float:left;width:180px;text-align:left}
nav ul li a {padding-bottom:2px}
nav ul li a:hover {background-color:lightblue;color:white}
```

Figure 19.15 CSS for <nav> element

a) State why this code uses descendant selectors. (1)
b) State the size of each box in the navigation bar. (1)
c) Describe precisely where the link text will be positioned with n each of the navigation boxes. (2)
d) Explain why the colour of the navigation boxes does not change when the mouse pointer passes over them. (1)
e) Explain why only the text is clickable and not the whole box for each link. (1)

6 Using the wireframe design for a navigation bar, shown in Figure 19.16, write the CSS code required to style the navigation bar. (5)

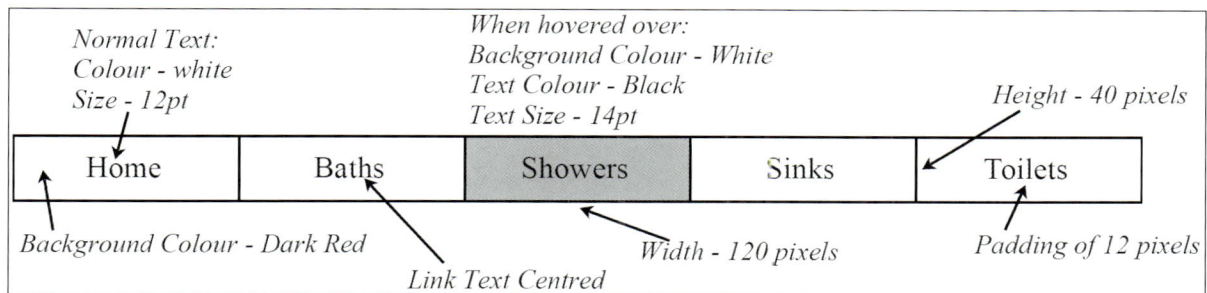

Figure 19.16 Wireframe for <nav> element

7 Using an editor of your choice (there are several free editors you can download to use at home like Notepad++ and Brackets), write the HTML form code to produce the example form design shown in the previous chapter (page 96). (8)

For each of the questions below describe the purpose of the JavaScript code.

8 (2)

```
<img src="boat.jpg"
onMouseOver="this.style.width='75px';this.style.height='75px'"
onMouseOut="this.style.width='150px';this.style.height='150px'">
```

Figure 19.17

9 (2)

```
<img id="speedboat" src="boat034.jpg"
onMouseOver="document.getElementById('sailingboat').style.
margin-top='25px'">
<img id="sailingboat" src="boat036.jpg" style="margin-top:0px">
```

Figure 19.18

⇒

⇨

10 (4)

```
<script>
function makeChange() {
document.getElementById('change').style.color='green';
document.getElementById('change').style.fontFamily='verdana'
}
</script>

<p id="change" onMouseOver="makeChange()"> Hello </p>
```

Figure 19.19

## Chapter 20

Web testing

Low-fidelity prototypes

Prototypes may be used to perform dry runs of a website design before implementation. Testers use the paper versions as if they were a real site. For example, when the tester pretends to click on a link, the next prototype page would be placed in front of the testers.

To improve the realism of the testing, the testers can be given:

- different tasks to complete such as finding information or a page within the website
- different personas such as experienced older users or young users familiar with hardware but not the website.

Forms

If a web page contains a form, then all the validation should be tested. A comprehensive test plan will include testing for:

- length of text input (maxlength)
- range of numeric input (min, max)
- multiple input options on drop-down menus (multiple)
- presence checks (required).

Navigation

A finished website should be tested thoroughly to ensure all the hyperlinks within the navigation bar work as intended. Any hyperlinks within page content should also be tested.

Media

Any images, sounds and videos within pages should be tested to ensure they can be viewed or played.

Platforms

When complete, the website should be tested using a variety of browsers and devices (tablets, smartphones and desktops). Code sometimes requires specific browser versions or plug-ins to display correctly.

What you should know 👍

In your revision of this chapter, ensure that you are able to:

- ★ explain the need for testing
- ★ describe a variety of tests conducted on websites
- ★ create a comprehensive test plan for an HTML form.

Questions ?

1 Using the example Form code from the previous chapter (Figure 19.12, page 96), devise a comprehensive test plan that could be used to ensure the 'attraction tickets' form works as intended. (6)

2 A company wishes to start a new online shop selling video games for consoles. Create three personas that could be used to test the website's low-fidelity prototype designs. (3)

Fitness for purpose

A website is said to be fit for purpose if it meets the functional requirements identified at the analysis stage. Functional requirements may include statements like:

- display the shark image on the diving page
- play required video on changing a bicycle tyre
- allow the user to search for products
- allow the user to login
- allow the user to purchase a product
- navigate to the external UN human rights website as required.

Usability

The usability of a website will be determined by factors such as:

- ease of navigation
- ease of searching for or finding content
- readability of the content
- clarity of images
- ease of use on different devices and screen sizes
- text-to-speech availability for visually impaired users.

Feedback gathered from testing or from surveying live users may help to evaluate usability.

Evaluation

When evaluating a website, the fitness for purpose should be discussed and a short report written on usability.

What you should know 👍

In your revision of this chapter, ensure that you are able to:

★ explain the term 'fit for purpose' in reference to websites
★ describe what factors affect the usability of websites.

Questions ❓

There are no questions for this chapter. It is recommended that you practise writing short evaluation reports on websites you have created during your lessons.

Assignment

## Chapter 22

Assignment preparation

The Higher course requires that you complete an 8-hour practical assignment in class. This is like a practical exam. The assignment has the following assessment conditions:

- It is an open-book assessment. You may use any previous examples of work that you created in lessons or search references online.
- You are not allowed to ask your teacher or your classmates for help.
- You should not discuss the tasks in or out of class.
- The evidence you create must be your own work. Sharing files or taking work home to complete will result in your evidence being invalid.
- Tasks may be completed in any order.

There are three main tasks in the assignment, one for each practical area. Below are some possible sub-tasks. For each area you will only be asked to complete some of these sub-tasks.

Possible database tasks

Analysis: You may be asked to read a scenario and identify end-user and functional requirements.

Design: You may be asked to complete an EOD or ERD from information you are given or to design a query.

Implementation: You will be supplied with a sample database that you will be expected to manipulate or query using SQL.

Testing: You may be given an SQL statement to test and comment on.

Evaluation: You may be asked to evaluate the database for fitness for purpose and accuracy of output.

Possible software (programming) tasks

Analysis: You may be asked to read a scenario and identify scope, boundaries or functional requirements.

Design: You may be asked to complete a main algorithm with data flow or you may be asked to refine part of a given algorithm.

Implementation: You will be supplied with a program design that you will be expected to code using Higher data structures and modular code with parameter passing. The problem will include the use of one or more standard algorithms. You may be required to read or write data to a .csv or .txt file.

Testing: You may be given test data to run and comment on. You may be asked to design your own test data.

Evaluation: You may be asked to evaluate your own code.

Possible web tasks

Analysis: You may be asked to read a scenario and identify end-user or functional requirements.

Design: You may be asked to complete a web structure diagram, a wireframe design for a page or to design a form.

Implementation: You will be supplied with an incomplete website. You will be given two or three tasks to complete, each of which will involve writing either HTML, CSS or JavaScript code.

Testing: You may be asked to test a form or devise a comprehensive test plan for a form on one of the website's pages.

Evaluation: You may be asked to evaluate the fitness for purpose or usability of the website.

Before the assignment

Ensure that you organise yourself before the assignment starts. Prepare examples of code, organise files in folders and create bookmarks to useful web pages.

Programming is a skill quickly lost if you have not done any for a while. Practise your coding (SQL, HTML, CSS, JavaScript and your programming languages) in the weeks before the exam.

During the assignment

Ensure you concentrate throughout the tasks. If you progress quickly, you will have more time to check your work later.

Use the checklist provided in the assignment to ensure that all your evidence is complete.

Keep your evidence organised. SQA markers can't mark work that you have lost or missed out of your evidence.

Answers to Chapter Questions

Chapter 1: Development methodologies

1 Changes/improvements can be suggested by the client throughout the process. (1)
2 Waterfall plans out the entire development cycle at the beginning. (1)
  Agile focuses on shorter-term planning of sub-projects. (1)
3 Testing in agile is conducted throughout development. (1)
4 Agile focuses time on fluid/adaptable development cycles rather than documenting each stage in detail. (1)
5 Waterfall – a charge control board (1); agile – sub-team members with input from client and managers (1).

Chapter 2: Software analysis

1 One mark each for:
   - Purpose – The employees will describe what the app should do.
   - Scope – The client/employees will agree what will be supplied at the end of the project.
   - Boundaries – The employees can provide precise details on the data to be stored.
   - Inputs, outputs and processes – The employees can describe what data should be entered for a concert and what they would like to view as output. This can help define the processes required. (4)
2 a) National survey team (1)
   b) It stores only the most common garden birds (1). The user enters a letter representing each bird and there are only 26 letters in the alphabet. (1)
   c) Greenfinch,GA3 7HS,29032019 (1)
   d) The loop where the birds are entered by the user runs until 9 is entered. (1)
3 Your answers should include:
   - Purpose – A description noting that the program will be used by guitar players to tune their guitars. (1)
   - Scope – A list of what will be delivered to the client, along with a timescale, similar to the example on page 6. (1)
   - Boundaries – The number of tuning combinations that will be stored, i.e. 5 (1). Whether your solution will run once or many times. (1)
   - Inputs – How the user selects the tuning (either type one in or offer a menu system) (1). The tuning data may also be input if it is stored in a file. (1)
   - Processes – Fetching the selected tuning notes. (1)
   - Output – The tuning for each of the six strings. (1)

Chapter 3: Software design

1 a) birdNames – array (1) of text variables (1)
      postcode – text variable (1)

$\Rightarrow$

⇨

birdData – array (1) of records (1) storing name, postcode and date (1)
numberOfSightings – integer variable (1)

   b) (i)   The process used to find the matching bird name is not fully explained. (1)

      (ii)   To enter each bird sighting (1) until 9 is entered (1).

      (iii)   The file is opened as 'write only'. Later data must be read from the file so a different connection is required.

   c) Lines 5 and 6 need to be redesigned as follows:

Step 5: Find a bird requested by user (IN: birdData(name,pcstcode,date), OUT: numberOfSightings, **firstDate, lastDate**) (1)

Step 6: Display **the requested bird information** (IN: numberOfSightings), **firstDate, lastDate**) (1)

2 There is no one answer for any algorithm refinement so a definitive answer is not given here. SQA mark these questions by using a checklist of refinements that must be included. One mark each (to a maximum of 5) for:

- ask the user if they wish to enter a concert
- input only occurs if the user answers yes (usually an IF statement)
- the user is asked for title, number of songs, each song title and the concert starting time
- a fixed loop is included for the number of songs entered by the user
- all the information is written to the file
- the file is opened (and maybe closed).

3 The answer below is written in pseudocode. This can be used to mark a structure diagram answer.

Step 1: Initialise variables and data structures. (1)

Step 2: Get selected tuning from user (OUT: tuningType, tuningPitch). (1)

Step 3: Find selected tuning (IN: tuningType, tuningPitch, tunings(type,pitch,strings), OUT: strings()). (1)

Step 4: Display selected tuning (IN: strings(), tuningType, tuningPitch). (1)

4 User interface answers can vary from student to student. SQA mark these questions using a checklist. Ensure your text or graphical design includes:

- inputs: tuningType, tuningPitch (1)
- instructions telling the user what to enter (1)
- outputs: type, pitch and strings (1).

Chapter 4: Software implementation

1 a) Global arrays: waitingDates, waitingTimes (1)

      Global variables: longestWait, minsWait, secsWait (1)

   b) waitingDates is an array of string variables (1)

      waitingTimes is an array of integer variables (1)

   c) Name of file: waitingTimes (1)

      Type of file: txt (1)

   d) Local variables – filetext, line (2)

      Formal parameters – dates, times (2)

   e) The function would take the time, which is stored as a string in the file (1), and convert this to an integer (1).

   f) secsWait: 6 (1)

      minsWait: 2 (1)

⇨

⇨

   g) The following should be included in the comment to describe the purpose of the procedure:
- display all the waiting times (1)
- for a date selected by the user (1).

2 A function returns a value, a procedure does not. (1)
3 Sub-string could be used to separate out each character (1).
   Each character could then be converted to an ASCII value (1).
   Subtracting 48 would convert the ASCII value to the actual number ('2' = ASCII value 50 − 48 = number 2) (1).
   Multiplying the first character by 10 and then adding the two numbers (1) would complete the conversion of text 25 to integer 25.
4 Note that your variable and array names may vary.

```
RECORD Actor IS {STRING name,  INTEGER age,  BOOLEAN member}
       (1)                (1)              (1)                (1)
DECLARE allActors AS ARRAY OF Actor INITIALLY [ ] * 50
         (1)                         (1)                (1)
```

Chapter 5: Standard algorithms

1 Each of the algorithms examines each element of an array in turn. (1)
2 Match your programming language to the SQARL answer below.

```
PROCEDURE displayLessThanThousand(ARRAY OF INTEGER times) (1)
     DECLARE countTimes AS INTEGER INITIALLY 0             (1)
     FOR counter FROM 0 TO length(times)-1 DO              (1)
          IF times [counter] < 1000 THEN                   (1)
               SET countTimes TO countTimes + 1            (1)
          END IF
     END FOR
     SEND countTimes TO DISPLAY                            (1)
END PROCEDURE
```

3 findMaxWaiting: find maximum (1); displayInfo: linear search (1)
4 The changes required to the algorithm are highlighted in bold. (3)

```
DECLARE earthquakeReadings INITIALLY
[3.4,6.3,2.9,7.6,5.5,1.8,4.2]
DECLARE minValue INITIALLY earthquakeReadings[0]
DECLARE position INITIALLY 0
FOR counter FROM 1 TO length(earthquakeReadings)-1 DO
IF earthquakeReadings[counter] < minValue THEN
          SET minValue TO earthquakeReadings[counter]
          SET position TO counter
END IF
END FOR
SEND ["The position of the smallest magnitude earthquake
was " & position] TO DISPLAY
```

Chapter 6: Software testing

1 a) Logic (1)
   b) Syntax (the name of function called does not exist) (1)
   c) Runtime (the user could potentially instigate a division by 0 by inputting 0) (1)

⇨

2 One mark for each correct value on the last line of the table. (4)
A trace table tracking the values of x, y, z and loop:

	x	y	z	loop
Line 1	0			
Line 2	0	2		
Line 3 (1st iteration of loop)	0	2		1
Line 4 (1st iteration of loop)	0	2	3	1
Line 5 (1st iteration of loop)	3	2	3	1
Line 3 (2nd iteration of loop)	3	2	3	2
Line 4 (2nd iteration of loop)	3	2	7	2
Line 5 (2nd iteration of loop)	7	2	7	2
Line 3 (3rd iteration of loop)	7	2	7	3
Line 4 (3rd iteration of loop)	7	2	12	3
Line 5 (3rd iteration of loop)	12	2	12	3

3 A breakpoint can be added after the first line of the calculation allowing the tester to check the calculation manually up to this point (1). If it is correct, the breakpoint may be moved to after the next line. This may be repeated until the line of code causing the error is found. (1)
4 A watchpoint (1) may be set up to stop the program with the condition sensor1>100 AND sensor3>100 (1). When the program stops, the value of sensor2 may be checked. (1)
5 The programmer is performing dry runs as they type, read and predict the effect of running their code.

Chapter 8: Data representation

1 a) 31 (1)
  b) −101 (1)
  c) 127 (1)
  d) −33 (1)
2 a) 0111 1010 (1)
  b) 1000 0111 (1)
  c) 0101 1011 (1)
  d) 1111 0100 (1)
3 a) −15 741 (1)
  b) −16 330 (1)
4 a) 0101 1110 0110 0001 (1)
  b) 1000 0100 1110 1111 (1)
5 a) (1)

+/−	mantissa															exponent (two's complement)							
0	1	0	1	1	0	1	0	1	0	0	0	0	0	0	0	0	0	0	0	0	1	0	0

b) (1)

1	1	1	1	0	0	1	0	0	1	1	0	1	0	1	0	0	0	0	0	0	1	1	0

c) (1)

0	1	0	0	1	0	1	1	0	0	0	0	0	0	0	0	1	1	1	1	1	1	1	0

⇨

d) (1)

1	1	1	0	1	0	1	0	1	1	0	0	0	0	0	0	1	1	1	1	1	1	0	0

6 The range of numbers would increase due to the larger exponent. (1)
The precision of numbers would decrease due to the smaller mantissa. (1)

7 Advantage: significantly larger range of characters available. (1)
Disadvantage: twice the storage is required for each character. (1)

8 Bit-mapped graphics application. (1)
Some pixels in the back photo were lost when the other photo was moved away, suggesting no layering. (1)

9 Printed at 800 dpi. (1)
Vector graphics are resolution independent so are displayed/printed at the resolution of the device. (1)

Chapter 9: Computer structure

1 The address bus is used to locate the program instruction in memory. (1)
The data bus is used to transfer the instruction from memory to the processor. (1)

2 L2 is a type of cache memory. (1)

3 The processor can be fatally damaged by constant over-clocking, often due to the excess heat produced. (1)

4 Number of processors; threading is a term most associated with running processes simultaneously or multi-core processors. (1)

Chapter 11: Security risks and precautions

1 A tracking cookie (1)

2 Denial of service attack (1)

3 The keys are paired as one key provides the means to unencrypt data encrypted using the other key. (1)

4 Ensure that the key is contained within a verified public certificate. (1)

Chapter 12: Database analysis

1 functional (1)

2 end-user (1)

3 functional (1)

4 functional (1)

5 functional (1)

6 end-user (1)

Chapter 13: Database design

1 Many-to-many relationships create excessive duplication of data (1). They should be split into two one-to-many relationships. (1)

⇨

⇨

2 (1)

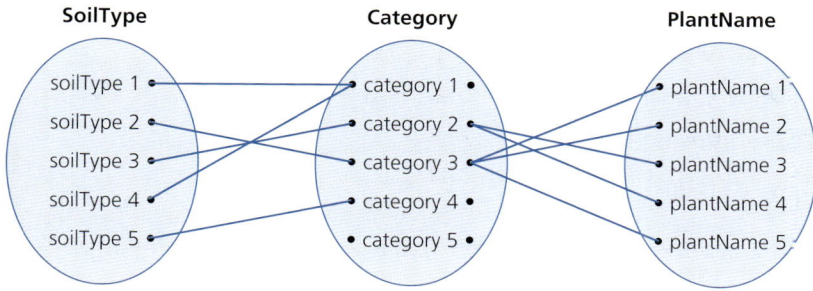

SoilType	Category	PlantName
soilType 1	category 1	plantName 1
soilType 2	category 2	plantName 2
soilType 3	category 3	plantName 3
soilType 4	category 4	plantName 4
soilType 5	category 5	plantName 5

3 SoilType – Category – 1-M (1)

Category – PlantName – 1-M (1)

4 One mark each (labels used may vary in your answer) for: (7)

- four correct entities
- correct attributes for Customer (address may be one attribute)
- correct attributes for OrderItem
- correct attributes for Order
- correct attributes for Item
- correct relationships
- correct cardinality.

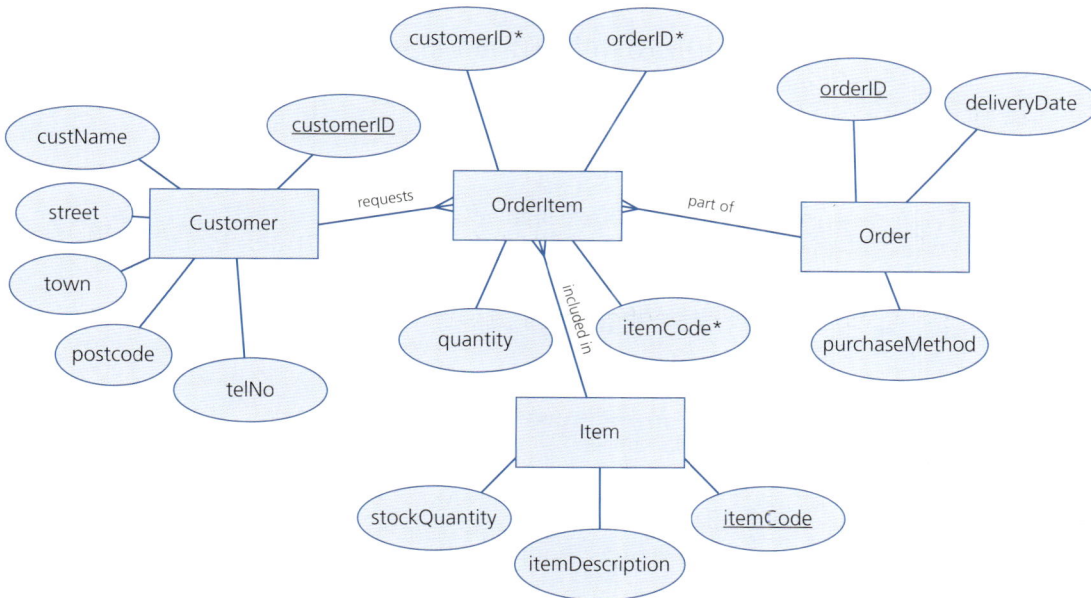

5 A compound key could be created (1) comprised of customerID, orderID and itemCode (1).

6 One mark for each correct table row in each answer.

a) (3)

	Answer
Field(s) and calculation(s)	memberName, Member.telNo
Table(s) and query	Member, Class
Search criteria	Class.classID = 35
	memberName LIKE "%Smith"
Grouping	
Sort order	

⇨

⇨

b) (4)

	Answer
Field(s) and calculation(s)	title, duration, fitnessPoints
Table(s) and query	Trainer, Class, ClassType
Search criteria	trainerName = "Brian Clark"
	classDate = "30/11/2019"
	classTime < "12:00"
Grouping	
Sort order	fitnessPoints (descending)

c) (4)

	Answer
Field(s) and calculation(s)	memberName, Member.telNo
Table(s) and query	Member, Class, ClassType
Search criteria	classDate = "02/01/2018"
	title LIKE "%Spinning%"
Grouping	
Sort order	memberName (ascending)

d) (3)

	Answer
Field(s) and calculation(s)	Classes Attended = COUNT(Attendance.memberID)
Table(s) and query	Member, Attendance, Class
Search criteria	classDate LIKE "%/2017"
	memberName = "Katie Bradley"
Grouping	
Sort order	

e) (4)

	Answer
Field(s) and calculation(s)	trainerName, Average Fitness Points = AVG(fitnessPoints)
Table(s) and query	Trainer, ClassType
Search criteria	trainerName = "Ploy Chandra"
Grouping	trainerName
Sort order	

f) (3)

	Answer
Field(s) and calculation(s)	trainerName, COUNT(Attendance.MemberID)
Table(s) and query	Trainer, Class, Attendance
Search criteria	
Grouping	trainerName
Sort order	

⇨

g) (6)

Query1	Answer
Field(s) and calculation(s)	expensive = MAX(cost)
Table(s) and query	ClassType
Search criteria	
Grouping	
Sort order	

Query2	Answer
Field(s) and calculation(s)	memberID, memberName
Table(s) and query	Member, ClassType, Query1
Search criteria	cost = expensive
Grouping	memberID
Sort order	

h) (6)

Query1	Answer
Field(s) and calculation(s)	memberID, telNo, totalPoints = SUM(fitnessPoints)
Table(s) and query	Member, ClassType
Search criteria	
Grouping	memberID, telNo
Sort order	

Query2	Answer
Field(s) and calculation(s)	Query1.memberID, Query1.telNo
Table(s) and query	Query1
Search criteria	totalPoints = 0
Grouping	
Sort order	

Chapter 14: Database implementation

One mark for each line of correct SQL.

1 (3)

```
UPDATE Member
SET street = '6 Woodburn Terrace', Member.telNo =
'07964388472'
WHERE memberName = 'Joyce Bryant';
```

2 (3)

```
SELECT title, levels
FROM ClassType
WHERE description LIKE "%no breaks%";
```

⇨

3 Note: Derek's name is not required in the statement search criteria as we are told there is only one class on at that date and time. (6)

```
SELECT durationMin/60*hourlyRate AS [payment for class]
FROM Trainer, Class, ClassType
WHERE classDate = '29/12/2018'
AND classTime = '10:00'
AND Trainer.trainerID = Class.trainerID
AND Class.typeID = ClassType.typeID;
```

4 (8)

```
SELECT memberName, AVG(fitnessPoints)
FROM Member, Attendance, Class, ClassType
WHERE memberName = "Zubair Samuels"
AND classDate LIKE '%/2018'
AND Attendance.memberID = Member.memberID
AND Class.classID = Attendance.classID
AND Class.typeID = ClassType.typeID
GROUP BY memberName;
```

5 (7)

```
SELECT memberName, MAX(cost) AS [Most Expensive],
MIN(cost) AS Cheapest
FROM Member, Attendance, Class, ClassType
WHERE memberName = "Jean Smith"
AND Attendance.memberID = Member.memberID
AND Class.classID = Attendance.classID
AND Class.typeID = ClassType.typeID
GROUP BY memberName;
```

6 (6)

```
SELECT Class.classID, title, COUNT(Attendance.memberID)
FROM Attendance, Class, ClassType
WHERE Class.classID = Attendance.classID
AND Class.typeID = ClassType.typeID
GROUP BY Class.classID, title
ORDER BY COUNT(Attendance.memberID) DESC;
```

7 Note that there may be other solutions to this. (9)

Query1

```
SELECT SUM(durationMin) AS totalTime
FROM Trainer, Class, ClassType
WHERE trainerName = "Robert Hightower"
AND classDate LIKE "%/03/2019"
AND Trainer.trainerID = Class.trainerID
AND Class.typeID = ClassType.typeID;
```

⇨

⇨

Query2

```
SELECT totalTime/60*hourlyRate AS [Payment]
FROM Trainer, Query1
WHERE  trainerName = "Robert Hightower";
```

8 The SQL statement would display the title and levels (1) of the fitness classes taken by trainer Bo Jackson (1).

9 The SQL statement would display the title and dates (1) of the fitness classes attended by members with the forename Jill (1).

10 The SQL statement would display each member's ID, name (1) and the total time they have spent in fitness classes (1).

Chapter 15: Database testing

One mark for each bullet point below:

1 ● The record for the intermediate spinning class should be examined to check the current duration and cost.
   ● The SQL statement should be run and the same values checked again to ensure they have changed.

2 ● The Class table should be checked and a manual count made of the number of times each trainerID appears.
   ● The SQL statement should then be run and the values checked against the manual count to see if they are the same.

3 ● The SQL statement displays the members that attended classID 5 so the database tables should be used to look up this information manually.
   ● The members' names found should then be written down in alphabetical order.
   ● The SQL statement should be run and the actual output compared to the manual list of names.

4 ● The cost has been changed to 10% of the original cost and not cost + 10%.
   ● Other classes beginning with 'S' may also be accidentally changed.

5 ● The wrong average is being calculated; it should be AVG(cost).
   ● Grouping the output would calculate the average for each class individually and not the average of all the classes as required. No grouping should be used.

6 ● The statement does not calculate the total money collected from each member, just the single cost of the class.
   ● There may be two classes on at the same date and time.

7 ● "memberID" is in two tables so the table must be identified: Member.memberID = 23.
   ● The Attendance table should be included in FROM.

8 ● Grouping must include every field (other than the aggregate function) in SELECT. GROUP BY trainerID, trainerName.
   ● The second join refers to classID. This should be trainerID.

9 ● The first AND should be WHERE.
   ● The ORDER and GROUP clauses are the wrong way round.

(Well done if you spotted there are two semi-colons in the statement.)

⇨

⇨

Chapter 16: Database evaluation
1 A Boolean (1) payment field (1) could be added to the Attendance table (1).
2 The database might now be required to produce new output (a new functional requirement) which it is incapable of producing without changes to the tables. (1)

Chapter 17: Web analysis
1 Requirements can be subjective so your answers may vary.
For end-user requirements, your answers should include anything that the customers (as they will be the end users) would like to see in the websiste, for example:
● pictures showing what each product looks like
● the cost of every item for sale on the website. (1)

For functional requirements, your answers should reflect what the website code will have to do:
● the website should have a home page and four main sub-pages: sinks, toilets, baths and showers
● each page should display pictures of products
● a video, showing the functions of the bath, should play on the whirlpool baths page. (1)

Chapter 18: Web design
1 A wireframe focuses on providing examples of page layouts. (1)
2 The main sub-pages shown on a website structure diagram (1) will become the hyperlinks in the navigation bar (1).
3 a) Drop-down menus and radio buttons. (2)
  b) Radio buttons. (1)
4 The text area can be coded with a default value that would be entered, as the required input, if the value wasn't changed by the user. (1)
5 The developer would discuss what the client didn't like about the design (1) and then redesign the website (1).

Chapter 19: Web implementation
1 One mark for each line of code:
```
header, nav, footer {padding:5px; font-size:12px}
main {padding:20px; font-size:10px}
```

2 a) The most efficient way to create a gap at every side is to add padding to the main element.
● main {padding:10px} (2)

⇨

⇨

  b) There are many combinations of this that can be written with styles applied to the different sections:

- #electric {margin-left:305px} – if the #complete <section> is floated, the margin of the #electric <section> pushes against the left edge of the <main> element as if the floated element was not there. The margin must be the width of the 300px section + 5 pixel space to position it. (1)
- #enclosures {margin-top:5px} – this margin could also be applied to the bottom of #complete or #electric <section> elements. (1)

  c) The text is closer to the edge of the container than the image so the space cannot be created using padding alone. Therefore, a margin must have been used to create the additional space. (1)

3 Float must be implemented on the following:
- the main title 'Bathroom Supplies for All'
- pedestal01.jpg
- wallMounted01.jpg
- either the pedestal sinks section (float:left) or the wall-mounted sinks section (float:right). (4)

4
- The 'Advantages' text below shower01.jpg and shower02.jpg – to ensure the text starts below the images. (1)
- The #enclosures <section> to cancel the effects of the floated sections above. (1)

5
  a) To ensure the styles are only applied to the <ul> list within the <nav>. (1)
  b) 180 px by 50 px (2)
  c) The text will be on the left (1), two pixels up from the bottom (1).
  d) The background colour and the hover colour are the same. (1)
  e) The code "display:block" should be included in the styles for the nav ul li a{} selector. (1)

6 One mark for each correct line of CSS. (5)

```
nav {height:40px;background-color:darkRed;font-size:12pt}
nav ul {list-style-type:none}
nav ul li {float:left;width:120px;text-align:center}
nav ul li a {display:block;padding:12px;color:white}
nav ul li a:hover {background-color:white;font-size:12pt;color:black}
```

7
- User instructions included (1)
- Submit button (1)
- Inputs
  - name: maxlength= "20", value="anonymous" and required set (1)
  - event: default added to track&field using "selected" (1)
  - rating: range added – min="1", max="10" and required set (1)
  - text area: 180 characters (could be three rows, 60 columns or another combination) (1)
  - radio buttons: default set to No using "checked" (1)
  - parking cost: min= "0", value= "0" and required set (1)

⇨

```
<form action="">
    Enter your name or stay anonymous if your prefer<br>
    <input type="text" name="name" size="20" maxlength="20" value="anonymous" required>
    <br><br>

    Which event did you attend?<br>
    <select name="event" size="4">
        <option value="track" selected>Track/Field</option>
        <option value="cycling">Cycling</option>
        <option value="rowing">Rowing</option>
        <option value="hockey">Hockey</option>
        <option value="football">Football</option>
        <option value="archery">Archery</option>
    </select>
    <br><br>

    Rate the venue you attended.<br>
    (Very Poor 0, Average 5, Excellent 10) <br>
    <input type="number" name="rating" min="1" max="10" required>
    <br><br>

    Describe any improvements that could be made to the venue.<br>
    <textarea name="improve" rows="3" cols="60"> </textarea>
    <br><br>

    Choose your ticket type:<br>
    <input type="radio" name="type" value="day" checked> day
    <input type="radio" name="type" value="week"> week
    <input type="radio" name="type" value="year"> year
    <br><br>

    How much did your parking cost? <br>
    £<input type="number" name="rating" min="0" value="0" required>
    <br><br>

    <input type="submit" value="Submit">
</form>
```

8 When the mouse is dragged over the boat.jpg image, the size of the image will be set to 75 × 75 pixels. (1)
   When the mouse is moved away from the boat.jpg image, the size of the image will be set to 150 × 150 pixels. (1)

9 When the mouse is moved over the boat034.jpg image (1), the margin at the top of the second image is increased from 0 to 25 px, (1).

10 When the mouse is moved over the word Hello (1), a function is called (1). The function sets the text colour to green (1) and the font to Verdana (1).

Chapter 20: Web testing

1 One mark for each bullet (to a maximum of 6):
   ● Test the maximum number of characters on each text input (firstname=15, surname=15).
   ● Test that multiple attractions can be selected from the drop-down menu.
   ● Test that the minimum and maximum number of tickets that can be entered are 1 and 8.
   ● Test that each radio button can be selected.
   ● Test that the text area accepts up to 100 characters.
   ● Test that the firstname and surname inputs cannot be left empty.

2 One mark for each persona to a maximum of 3 marks. As games can only be sold to certain age groups, the personas should have a range of ages corresponding to game ratings.